Uses of Numbers

Tell how each number is being used. Write *position*, *cou...*, *measure*, or *label* for each.

> **Jennifer lives at 349 Ridge Meadow.**
>
> The number 349 is used to **label** or identify Jennifer's house.

1. Michael wears a size 8 pair of tennis shoes.

   _____

2. Emily read 35 pages of her new book.

   _____

3. John's team had 3 home runs in the game.

   _____

4. Jason's phone number is 331-2525.

   _____

5. Jenny needs 12 feet of fencing for the pen.

   _____

6. Cab #321 picked us up at the airport.

   _____

7. Pete was the sixth person in line to get tickets.

   _____

8. The puppy weighed 8 pounds.

   _____

9. The 747 airplane is roomy and seats a lot of passengers.

   _____

10. Jeff got a score of 90% on his math test.

    _____

11. The winter storm was the first of the season.

    _____

12. The singing group's name is *Wink 133*.

    _____

13. The plane arrived at Gate 8.

    _____

14. A large bag contains 50 mints.

    _____

Problem Solving

15. Identify the number used to measure in the statement below.

    There are 45 students in our school on the track team. At our first meet, Jana came in second in the 200-meter dash.

    _____

Use with text pages 4–5.

Place Value Through Hundred Thousands

Write each number in three other ways.

> **328 thousand, 514**
>
> **Word form:** three hundred twenty-eight thousand, five hundred fourteen
>
> **Expanded form:** 300,000 + 20,000 + 8,000 + 500 + 10 + 4
>
> **Standard form:** 328,514

1. 246,718

2. 300,000 + 40,000 + 2,000 + 100 + 50 + 9

_____

_____

_____

_____

_____

_____

_____

_____

Write the value of the underlined digit.

3. 76,9<u>8</u>2 _____

4. 6<u>6</u>,424 _____

5. 925,7<u>3</u>3 _____

Algebra • Equations Find each missing number.

6. 7,000 + ■ + 40 + 5 = 7,845

7. ■ + 8,000 + 900 + 70 + 6 = 18,976

8. 200,000 + 40,000 + 5,000 + 700 + ■ + 3 = 245,783

Problem Solving

9. What is the value of the hundred thousands digit in the number 178,632?

_____

Use with text pages 6–9.

Problem-Solving Strategy:
Use Logical Reasoning

Use logical reasoning to solve each problem.

Blaine, Jorge, Una, and Casey are standing in line. Una is not first. Blaine is fourth. Jorge is directly behind Casey. List the four friends in order from first to fourth.

Use a chart. Fill in what you know. Then use Logical Reasoning to fill in the rest of the chart.

	First	Second	Third	Fourth
Blaine	no	no	no	yes
Jorge	no	yes	no	no
Una	no	no	yes	no
Casey	yes	no	no	no

The four friends in order from first to fourth are Casey, Jorge, Una, Blaine.

---

1. Ben, Margaret, Tyler, and Jessie are playing a game where they take turns. Tyler did not go last. Jessie went immediately after Ben. Margaret went first. In what order did the players take their turns?

_____

2. Belle, Sebastian, Roy, and May each chose soccer, football, basketball, or baseball as their favorite sport. No two of them chose the same sport. Sebastian does not like soccer or football. Roy does not like soccer. May does not like basketball. Belle chose baseball. What is each person's favorite sport?

_____

Use with text pages 10–12.

How Big Is One Million?

Use the chart to answer the following questions.

$1 \times 1{,}000{,}000 = 1{,}000{,}000$ ⟶	1 times 1 million = 1 million
$10 \times 100{,}000 = 1{,}000{,}000$ ⟶	10 times 1 hundred thousand = 1 million
$100 \times 10{,}000 = 1{,}000{,}000$ ⟶	100 times 10 thousand = 1 million
$1{,}000 \times 1{,}000 = 1{,}000{,}000$ ⟶	1,000 times 1 thousand = 1 million
$10{,}000 \times 100 = 1{,}000{,}000$ ⟶	10,000 times 1 hundred = 1 million
$100{,}000 \times 10 = 1{,}000{,}000$ ⟶	100,000 times ten = 1 million
$1{,}000{,}000 \times 1 = 1{,}000{,}000$ ⟶	1,000,000 times 1 = 1 million

How many tens are in 1,000,000?

Chart shows 100,000 times ten = 1 million.

There are 100,000 tens in 1,000,000.

1. How many ones are there in 1,000,000? _____

2. How many hundreds are there in 1,000,000? _____

3. How many hundred thousands are there in 1,000,000? _____

4. How many ten thousands are there in 1,000,000? _____

5. How many thousands are there in 1,000,000? _____

Use the chart to complete these problems.

6. $1{,}000 \times$ _____ $= 1{,}000{,}000$ 7. $10 \times$ _____ $= 1{,}000{,}000$

8. $100 \times$ _____ $= 1{,}000{,}000$ 9. $10{,}000 \times$ _____ $= 1{,}000{,}000$

Problem Solving

10. Jack has 5,000,000 pennies. If each roll holds 50 pennies, how many rolls will Jack need for all the pennies?

_____

4   **Use with text pages 14–15.**

Order Numbers

Write the numbers in order from least to greatest.

> **84,298, 83,199, and 85,365.**
>
> 83,199
> 84,298
> 85,365
>
> 5 is the greatest digit, so 85,365 is the greatest number.
>
> 83,199
> 84,298
> 3 < 4 so 83,199 is the least.
>
> 83,199   84,298   85,365

1. 6,200   2,060   6,002

2. 10,188   11,351   9, 465

_____

_____

Write the numbers in order from greatest to least.

3. 17,566   17,466   17,664

4. 37,115   37,151   36,864

_____

_____

Problem Solving

Show your work.

5. In 2003, the Summer Smash Festival had 148,982 attendees. In 2004, the festival had 151,382 attendees. In 2005, the festival had 148,442 attendees. Order the numbers from least to greatest.

_____

Use with text pages 26–28.

Compare and Order Money

Compare the amount below to $100.

$50.00 → $70.00 → $90.00 → $95.00 → $96.00 → 25¢ → 50¢ → 51¢ → 61¢ → 66¢

Write the total amount as $96.66.
Then compare $96.66 to $100.

Solution: $96.66 < $100

Write each amount. Then write the greater amount.

1.  **or**

_____

2. 11 quarters, 8 dimes, 3 nickels   **or**   8 quarters, 11 dimes, 9 nickels

_____

3. 9 one-dollar bills, 17 quarters   **or**   2 five-dollar bills, 3 one-dollar bills

_____

Problem Solving

Show your work.

4. Frank wants to buy a fabric for his art
project. The fabric costs $11.95. Frank
has 1 five-dollar bill, 6 one-dollar bills,
3 quarters, and 3 dimes. Does Frank
have enough money? Why or why not?

_____

8   **Use with text pages 30–32.**

Problem-Solving Application:
Use a Bar Graph

The Mineola Elementary School is having
an art show. The bar graph shows how
many students from each grade
participated in the art show.

**How many students are in the grade
that had about half as many students
participating as Grade 4?**

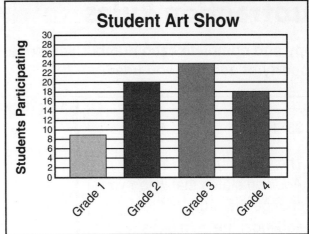

UNDERSTAND
You can use the height of the bars on the graph to
compare the number of students from each grade.

PLAN
Find the bar that is about half as tall as the bar for Grade 4.
What is the label for that bar?

_____

SOLVE
How many students participated for Grade 4?

_____

How many students participated for Grade 1?

_____

LOOK BACK
Look back at the problem.
How could you check to see if your answer is reasonable?

_____

1. Which grade had the most students
   participating?

2. How many more students from Grade
   3 participated than students from
   Grade 4?

_____   _____

11   **Use with text pages 40–43.**

Addition Properties and Subtraction Rules

Copy and complete each number sentence. Tell which property of addition you used.

35 + 51 = _____ + 35
The *Commutative Property of Addition* states that when you change the order of the addends, the sum stays the same.
35 + 51 = $\underline{51}$ + 35
86 = 86
The missing number is 51.

1. (15 + 7) + 23 = 15 +

_____

2. 542 + 0 =

_____

3. (27 + 18) + 13 = 27 +

_____

4. 84 + 61 = 61 +

_____

5. 0 + 753 =

_____

Use the Associative Property to help you find each sum mentally.

6. 85 + 61 + 15

_____

7. 93 + 25 + 75

_____

8. 151 + 62 + 49

_____

9. 422 + 345 + 78

_____

10. 575 + 94 + 106

_____

11. 84 + 165 + 35

_____

Problem Solving

12. Helena read 67 pages of a book on Monday. On Tuesday, she read 98 pages of the book. On Wednesday, she read the remaining 33 pages of the book. How many pages were in the book?

Show your work.

_____

Use with text pages 60–61.

Mental Math Strategies

Use mental math to add or subtract.

---

99 + 78

Use compensation.

Add 1 to 99 to make 100.

100 + 78 = 178

Subtract 1 to compensate.

178 − 1 = 177

99 + 78 = 177

---

1. 82 + 31

_____

2. 65 + 14

_____

3. 69 + 46

_____

4. 663 + 248

_____

5. 87 − 61

_____

6. 357 − 28

_____

7. 362 + 247

_____

Compare. Write >, <, or = for each ◯.

8. 63 + 87 ◯ 83 + 67

9. 31 + 74 ◯ 30 + 76

10. 95 − 32 ◯ 92 − 36

11. 236 − 57 ◯ 231 − 52

12. 642 + 158 ◯ 639 + 160

13. 507 − 96 ◯ 189 + 221

Problem Solving

14. Julie collected 163 miniature cars. She traded 32 old ones for 22 new ones. How many miniature cars does she have now?

Show your work.

_____

Use with text pages 62–63.

Estimate Sums and Differences

**Round each number to the nearest hundred or dollar.
Then estimate.**

```
562 + 311
   562  rounds to      600
  +311  rounds to     +300
                       900

562 + 311 is about 900.
```

1. 627 − 194

2. 722 + 236

3. 951 − 503

_____   _____   _____

4.   8,376
       − 584

5. $562.34
       −$166.12

6.   3,229
       +5,287

7. $29.68
       +$58.79

Round each number to the nearest ten. Then estimate.

8.   5,328
       − 784

9.   6,821
       −3,689

10.   942
        +368

11.   61,358
        + 9,513

Round each number to the greatest place. Then estimate.

12. 6,874 + 804

13. 9,384 − 6,284

14.   3,842
        + 690

15.   6,324
         2,895
        +2,358

Problem Solving

16. Mark listened to three CDs. The first one
was 72 minutes long. The second one
was 58 minutes long. The third one was
63 minutes long. About how many total
minutes of music did Mark listen to?

Show your work.

_____

Use with text pages 64–67.

Problem-Solving Decision: Estimate or Exact Answer

Solve. Tell whether you need an exact answer or an estimate.

The Burlington Elementary School had a general assembly of all students at the school. The students were seated according to what grade they were in. The table shows how many students attended from each grade.

Student Assembly	
Grade	**Number of Students**
1	116
2	98
3	162
4	139

How many more fourth-grade students than second-grade students attended the assembly?

Plan: I have to subtract to find out "how many more."

$$\begin{array}{r} \overset{013}{\cancel{1}\cancel{3}9} \\ -\ 98 \\ \hline 41 \end{array}$$

The question asks how many more. I need an exact answer.

So, 41 more fourth-grade students than second-grade students attended the assembly.

1. About how many students attended the general assembly altogether?

   Hint: Check the wording of the question. Do you need an exact answer or an estimate?

   _____

   Show your work.

2. After the first half of the assembly, the first-graders were sent back to class. How many students were left attending the general assembly?

   _____

Use with text pages 68–69.

Name _____ Date _____

Add Whole Numbers

Add.

2,874 + 957	Check by estimating.
1 1 1	2,847 → 3,000
2,874	+ 957 +1,000
+ 957	4,000
3,831	
Regroup if the sum of the digits in a place value is 10 or greater.	3,831 is close to 4,000. The answer is reasonable.

1. 5,108
    +4,843

2. 1,753
    +4,637

3. 3,842
    +3,584

4. 2,884
    +4,067

5. $65.27
    +$19.21

6. $74.63
    +$32.08

7. $932.84
    + $60.88

8. $304.98
    +$632.84

9. 675 + 132 + 554

_____

10. 328 + 805 + 335

_____

11. 7,154 + 3,765 + 2,085

_____

12. 5,324 + 5,841 + 8,935

_____

13. 7,080 + 6,657 + 4,849

_____

14. 9,084 + 6,743 + 8,654

_____

Problem Solving

Show your work.

15. Galaxy Comics sold $783.43 worth of comic books on Friday, $823.98 on Saturday, and $992.48 on Sunday. What was the total amount sold over the three days?

_____

Use with text pages 70–71.

Subtract Whole Numbers

Subtract. Use addition or estimation to check.

3,745 − 849	Check by adding.
$\overset{16\ 13}{\overset{2\ \cancel{6}\ \cancel{3}15}{\cancel{3,745}}}$ − 849 ‾‾‾‾‾‾ 2,896	$\overset{1\ 11}{2,896}$ + 849 ‾‾‾‾‾ 3,745

If you cannot subtract the digits in a column, regroup from a larger place.

1. 5,378
  − 849

2. 7,235
  − 953

3. 8,135
  − 846

4. $224.86
  −$132.87

5. $912.25
  −$842.18

6. 9,354
  −7,889

7. 8,468 − 6,185

_____

8. 4,358 − 4,327

_____

9. 7,354 − 2,188

_____

10. $88.55 − $44.57

_____

11. $94.18 − $75.78

_____

12. $91.11 − $54.87

_____

Algebra • Equations Find each missing number.

13. 495 − 371 = _____

14. _____ + $54.95 = $178.83

15. 1,398 − _____ = 817

Problem Solving

16. A concert hall seats 2,342 people. If 1,973 people attended last night's concert, how many seats were unoccupied?

_____

Show your work.

Use with text pages 72–73.

Subtract Across Zeros

Subtract. Estimate or add to check.

$$7,002 - 594$$

Regroup one thousand as 10 hundreds, regroup one of those hundreds as 10 tens, and regroup one of those tens as 10 ones.

$$7,002 - 594 = 6,408$$

1. $\begin{array}{r} 4,000 \\ -\ \ 335 \\ \hline \end{array}$

2. $\begin{array}{r} 7,064 \\ -\ \ 499 \\ \hline \end{array}$

3. $\begin{array}{r} \$308.04 \\ -\$247.62 \\ \hline \end{array}$

4. $\begin{array}{r} \$500.07 \\ -\$321.15 \\ \hline \end{array}$

5. $\begin{array}{r} 8,301 \\ -5,584 \\ \hline \end{array}$

6. $\begin{array}{r} 5,084 \\ -2,290 \\ \hline \end{array}$

7. $7,004 - 2,840$

8. $6,102 - 3,354$

9. $5,320 - 2,299$

10. $\$60.00 - \$56.85$

11. $\$100.00 - \$81.54$

12. $\$50.00 - \$28.74$

Follow the rule to complete each table.

Rule: Add 5,489	
Input	Output
13.	7,005
189	5,678
14. 2,300	

Rule: Subtract 305	
Input	Output
15. 9,095	
16.	715
1,005	700

Rule: Subtract 1,549	
Input	Output
17. 4,023	
18. 5,900	
7,804	6,255

Problem Solving

Show your work.

19. A folk singer made 1,000 copies of his current CD. So far, he has sold 583 copies. How many copies does he have left?

Use with text pages 74–75.

Add and Subtract
Greater Numbers

Add or subtract. Estimate to check.

$$613,813 - 289,465 \quad \textbf{Check:}$$

$$
\begin{array}{r}
5\ ^{10}\cancel{013}\ 7\ ^{10}\cancel{013} \\
\cancel{613,813} \\
-289,465 \\
\hline
324,348
\end{array}
\qquad
\begin{array}{r}
11\quad 11 \\
324,348 \\
+289,465 \\
\hline
613,813
\end{array}
$$

$$613,813 - 289,465 = 324,348$$

1. $\begin{array}{r} 841,321 \\ -784,236 \\ \hline \end{array}$ **2.** $\begin{array}{r} 546,753 \\ -324,849 \\ \hline \end{array}$

3. $\begin{array}{r} \$844.09 \\ -\ \$78.95 \\ \hline \end{array}$ **4.** $\begin{array}{r} \$879.65 \\ -\$723.08 \\ \hline \end{array}$

5. $375,459 - 234,756$ **6.** $\$3,741.56 + \$6,083.52$ **7.** $\$3,744.73 - \$2,516.50$

_____   _____   _____

Find the missing digit.

8. $\begin{array}{r} 67,823 \\ +45,\_38 \\ \hline 113,361 \end{array}$ **9.** $\begin{array}{r} 42,318 \\ +38,765 \\ \hline 81,0\_3 \end{array}$ **10.** $\begin{array}{r} 74,\_85 \\ -66,881 \\ \hline 7,804 \end{array}$

_____   _____   _____

Compare. Write < , >, or = for each ◯.

11. $\$944.15 + \$605.05 \ \bigcirc \ \$1,405.20$ **12.** $896 - 745 \ \bigcirc \ 869 - 718$

Problem Solving

13. Frank earned $324.52 during his first week of work tiling floors. During his second week of work he earned $287.62. How much more did he earn during his first week of work?

Show your work.

_____

         Use with text pages 76–79.

Multiplication Properties and Division Rules

Solve. Name the multiplication properties that you use.

> **1 × 7 = _____**
>
> The *Property of One* states that when you multiply any number by one, the product is equal to that number.
>
> **1 × 7 = 7**

1. $6 \times 5 = 5 \times \blacksquare$ **2.** $(3 \times 7) \times 2 = 3 \times (\blacksquare \times 2)$

_____   _____

_____   _____

3. $0 \times 61 = \blacksquare$ **4.** $6 \times \blacksquare \times 1 = 1 \times 6 \times 3$ **5.** $(9 \times 2) \times 5 = 9 \times (2 \times \blacksquare)$

_____   _____   _____

_____   _____   _____

Solve. Explain the division rule that you use. If there is no solution, tell why.

6. $0 \div 71 = \blacksquare$ **7.** $\blacksquare \div 23 = 1$ **8.** $29 \div \blacksquare = 29$

_____   _____   _____

_____   _____   _____

_____   _____   _____

_____   _____   _____

Problem Solving

Show your work.

9. Henry had 8 soccer games this season. In each game, he scored 1 goal. How many goals did he score? Which property did you use?

_____

_____

20   **Use with text pages 84–87.**

Relate Multiplication and Division

Write the fact family for each array or set of numbers.

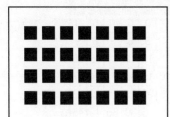

4 × 7 = 28

7 × 4 = 28

28 ÷ 7 = 4

28 ÷ 4 = 7

1. ● ● ● ● ● ● ● ●
● ● ● ● ● ● ●

_____

_____

_____

_____

2. ▪▪▪▪▪▪▪▪▪
▪▪▪▪▪▪▪▪▪
▪▪▪▪▪▪▪▪▪
▪▪▪▪▪▪▪▪▪

_____

_____

_____

_____

3. 3, 5, 15

_____

_____

_____

_____

4. 4, 8, 32

_____

_____

_____

_____

5. 3, 7, 21

_____

_____

_____

_____

Complete each fact family.

6. 6 × 4 = ▪   ▪ ÷ 6 = 4   **7.** 7 × 2 = ▪   ▪ ÷ 2 = 7

4 × ▪ = 24   24 ÷ ▪ − 6   2 × ▪ = 14   14 ÷ ▪ = 2

Problem Solving

8. There are 4 rows and 8 chairs in each row. What fact family can you write with this information?

_____

_____

_____

Use with text pages 88–89.

Patterns in Multiplication and Division

Multiplication	columns
The product of two numbers is shown in the table in the square where the row and column of the two factors meet.	

columns

×	0	1	2	3	4	5	6	7	8	9
0	0	0	0	0	0	0	0	0	0	0
1	0	1	2	3	4	5	6	7	8	9
2	0	2	4	6	8	10	12	14	16	18
3	0	3	6	9	12	15	18	21	24	27
4	0	4	8	12	16	20	24	28	32	36
5	0	5	10	15	20	25	30	35	40	45
6	0	6	12	18	24	30	36	42	48	54
7	0	7	14	21	28	35	42	49	56	63
8	0	8	16	24	32	40	48	56	64	72
9	0	9	18	27	36	45	54	63	72	81

rows

Division

To divide, find the row of the number that you are dividing by. Find the number you are dividing. Follow the column up to the top to find the quotient.

Use the multiplication table to answer each question.

1. Find the product of 3 and 7 in two places in the table. Describe where you found each product. Write two multiplication sentences using 3 and 7 as factors. What property do the number sentences show?

_____

_____

_____

2. Find the product of 5 and 9 in two places in the table. Describe where you found each product. Write two multiplication sentences using 5 and 9 as factors. What property do the number sentences show?

_____

_____

_____

3. Find 42 in two places in the table. If you divide 42 by the number of the row it is in, where can you find the quotient? Write two division sentences using both the row and the column numbers as divisors.

_____

4. Find 36 in three places in the table. Write three division sentences using both the row and the column numbers as divisors.

_____

_____

Use with text pages 90–91.

Name ______________________ Date ____________

Homework 4.4

Multiplication and Division Facts to Five

5 × 6	18 ÷ 6
Use Skip Counting	**Use a Related Multiplication Fact**
Think: 5, 10, 15, 20, 25, 30	**Think:** 18 ÷ 6 = ■
So 5 × 6 = 30.	6 × ■ = 18
	6 × 3 = 18
	So 18 ÷ 6 = 3.

Multiply or divide.

1. $\begin{array}{r} 3 \\ \times 6 \\ \hline \end{array}$

2. $\begin{array}{r} 8 \\ \times 2 \\ \hline \end{array}$

3. $\begin{array}{r} 4 \\ \times 4 \\ \hline \end{array}$

4. $\begin{array}{r} 7 \\ \times 5 \\ \hline \end{array}$

5. $5\overline{)30}$

6. $4\overline{)24}$

7. $3\overline{)21}$

8. $2\overline{)18}$

9. 5 × 8 ________

10. 2 × 9 ________

11. 45 ÷ 5 ________

12. 27 ÷ 3 ________

Problem Solving

Show your work.

13. Colored highlighter pens cost $3 per package. How many packages can you buy for $12?

____

Use with text pages 92–93.

Multiplication and Division Facts to Ten

Find 8 × 9.	Find 40 ÷ 8.
Use a Known Fact	**Use a Related Fact**
Think: 8 × 8 = 64 and 8 × 9 is one more group of 8, so	**Think:** 40 ÷ 8 = ▨
8 × 9 = 64 + 8	8 × ▨ = 40
8 × 9 = 72	8 × 5 = 40
	40 ÷ 8 = 5

Multiply or divide.

1. 8
   ×7

2. 6
   ×9

3. 6
   ×6

4. 7
   ×7

5. 7)63

6. 9)54

7. 8)72

8. 8)48

9. 10 × 9

10. 8 × 8

11. 6 × 7

12. 9 × 9

_____ _____ _____ _____

Compare. Write >, <, or = for each ◯.

13. 60 ÷ 10 ◯ 63 ÷ 9

14. 7 × 8 ◯ 6 × 9

15. 72 ÷ 8 ◯ 100 ÷ 10

Problem Solving

Show your work.

16. Daisy counted tarantula spiders at the zoo. She saw 56 legs in all. How many spiders did she see?

   Hint: Spiders have 8 legs.

_____

Use with text pages 94–97.

Multiply and Divide with 11 and 12

Multiplication

The product of two numbers is shown in the table in the square where the row and column of the two factors meet.

Division

To divide, find the row of the number that you are dividing by. Find the number you are dividing. Follow the column up to the top to find the quotient.

columns

×	0	1	2	3	4	5	6	7	8	9	10	11	12
0	0	0	0	0	0	0	0	0	0	0	0	0	0
1	0	1	2	3	4	5	6	7	8	9	10	11	12
2	0	2	4	6	8	10	12	14	16	18	20	22	24
3	0	3	6	9	12	15	18	21	24	27	30	33	36
4	0	4	8	12	16	20	24	28	32	36	40	44	48
5	0	5	10	15	20	25	30	35	40	45	50	55	60
6	0	6	12	18	24	30	36	42	48	54	60	66	72
7	0	7	14	21	28	35	42	49	56	63	70	77	84
8	0	8	16	24	32	40	48	56	64	72	80	88	96
9	0	9	18	27	36	45	54	63	72	81	90	99	108
10	0	10	20	30	40	50	60	70	80	90	100	110	120
11	0	11	22	33	44	55	66	77	88	99	110	121	132
12	0	12	24	36	48	60	72	84	96	108	120	132	144

rows

Multiply or divide. Use the table to help you.

1. 11×7

2. 12×9

3. 11×6

4. 12×8

5. $8)\overline{88}$

6. $11)\overline{99}$

7. $6)\overline{72}$

8. $12)\overline{48}$

9. $10 \times 11 =$

10. $11 \times 3 =$

11. $12 \times 11 =$

12. $12 \times 12 =$

_____   _____   _____   _____

13. $110 \div 10 =$

14. $84 \div 12 =$

15. $108 \div 12 =$

16. $121 \div 11 =$

_____   _____   _____   _____

Problem Solving

Show your work.

17. Steve's album is 72 minutes long. Each song on the album is 6 minutes long. How many songs are on the album?

_____

Use with text pages 98–99.

Multiply Three Factors

Use properties to show two different ways to multiply. Then find the product.

$5 \times 3 \times 4 =$ _____

You can use the **Associative Property** to group factors together.

You can multiply 5×3 first.	You can multiply 3×4 first.
$5 \times 3 \times 4 = $ ▨	$5 \times 3 \times 4 = $ ▨
$(5 \times 3) \times 4 = $ ▨	$5 \times (3 \times 4) = $ ▨
$\quad 15 \times 4 = 15 + 15 + 15 + 15 = 60$	$\quad \mathbf{5 \times 12 = 60}$
$\mathbf{5 \times 3 \times 4 = 60}$	

---

1. $4 \times 1 \times 3$ **2.** $6 \times 2 \times 2$ **3.** $9 \times 3 \times 3$ **4.** $4 \times 3 \times 2$

_____   _____   _____   _____

_____   _____   _____   _____

_____   _____   _____   _____

Find the missing number in each number sentence.

5. ▨ $\times 12 \times 9 = 0$ **6.** $11 \times 10 \times 1 = $ ▨   **7.** $8 \times 4 \times 3 = $ ▨

8. $(5 \times 6) \times $ ▨ $= 30$ **9.** $7 \times ($ ▨ $\times 7) = 98$ **10.** $($ ▨ $\times 7) \times 5 = 70$

Problem Solving

Show your work.

11. A box has 12 CD sets in it. Each set holds 4 CDs. How many CDs are in 5 boxes?

_____

     26   **Use with text pages 100–101.**

Division With Remainders

Divide. Write the remainder.

$$21 \div 4$$

Divide. Multiply, then subtract.

$$\begin{array}{r} 5\ R1 \\ 4\overline{)21} \\ -20 \\ \hline 1 \end{array}$$ ← Multiply. 4×5
← Subtract. $21 - 20$
This is the remainder.

$$21 \div 4 = 5\ R1$$

1. $5\overline{)29}$

2. $3\overline{)22}$

3. $7\overline{)31}$

4. $6\overline{)19}$

5. $2\overline{)15}$

6. $41 \div 7$

7. $52 \div 9$

_____   _____   _____

8. $35 \div 8$

9. $43 \div 5$

10. $28 \div 6$

_____   _____   _____

Solve.

11. $51 \div \blacksquare = 5\ R6$

12. $44 \div 5 = 8\ R\blacksquare$

13. $16 \div 3 = \blacksquare\ R1$

14. $\blacksquare \div 7 = 5$

15. $19 \div 4 = 4\ R\blacksquare$

16. $\blacksquare \div 2 = 5\ R1$

Problem Solving

Show your work.

17. Charlie is organizing books on his bookshelf. He owns 47 books. If he puts an equal number of books on 6 shelves, how many will fit on each shelf, and how many will be left over?

_____

Use with text pages 102–103.

Problem-Solving Decision: Choose the Operation

Solve. Explain why you chose each operation.

Miko has a collection of different computer games. The table at the right shows how many of each type of game Miko has.

Computer Games	
Type	**Number of Games**
Classic	8
First Person	12
Puzzle	9
Educational	6

How many computer games does Miko own?	**How many more First Person games does Miko have than Puzzle games?**
You *add* to find the total.	You *subtract* to find the difference.
8 + 12 + 9 + 6 = 35 games	12 − 9 = 3 games

1. The school library has five times as many Educational games as Miko does. How many Educational games are in the school library?

   _____

   _____

Show your work.

2. Miko trades 5 First Person games for 3 Classic games and 2 Educational games for 3 Puzzle games. How many games does Miko have now?

   _____

   _____

   _____

   _____

28

Use with text pages 104–105.

Order of Operations

Simplify. Follow the order of operations.

$7 + (12 \div 3) \times 5$

$7 + (12 \div 3) \times 5$ = Simplify inside parentheses.
$7 + 4 \times 5$ = Multiply and divide from left to right.
$7 + 20$ = Add and subtract from left to right.
27

1. $(7 + 8) \times 2$

2. $(12 - 7) \times 8$

3. $(9 + 7) \div 8$

_____

_____

_____

4. $25 + (4 \times 5) - 15$

5. $70 - (8 \times 5) \div 10$

6. $(28 - 4) \div 3$

_____

_____

_____

Copy the expression. Then insert parentheses to make 15.

7. $8 + 21 \div 3$

8. $12 + 18 \div 2$

9. $3 \times 9 - 4$

_____

_____

_____

Problem Solving

Show your work.

10. There are 30 students in the classroom. If three groups of 4 students leave the room, how many are left? How did you get your answer?

_____

_____

_____

Use with text pages 110–111.

Words Into Expressions

Kelly is researching the healing properties of garlic. She counted 12 cloves in each head of garlic. She counted 5 heads of garlic. How many cloves did she count?

Step 1: Let n stand for the number of heads of garlic.

You may choose any letter or symbol for the variable.

Step 2: Then express the number of cloves as

$$12 \times n \quad \text{or} \quad 12 \cdot n \quad \text{or} \quad 12n$$

You read all these expressions as "12 times n."

Step 3: $12n = 12 \times 5 = 60$

Simplify the expression.

She counted 60 cloves of garlic.

Write the expression. Let n stand for the number of relatives in Georgia's family.

1. 3 more relatives than in Georgia's family

2. One half as many relatives as in Georgia's family

_____   _____

Evaluate each expression when $c = 9$.

3. $7c$ 4. $c + 11$ 5. $3c - 5$ 6. $c \div 3$ 7. $2c + 7$

_____   _____   _____   _____   _____

Problem Solving

Show your work.

8. On Monday, 138 third-graders and 153 fourth-graders attended Hopatcong Elementary School. How many more fourth-graders attended than third-graders? Write an expression.

_____

Use with text pages 112–115.

Compare Expressions

Compare. Let $f = 11$. Write $=$ or $\neq$ for each $\bigcirc$.

$f + 21 \bigcirc 39 - f$

Step 1: Evaluate each expression.

$f + 21 \bigcirc 39 - f$

$11 + 21 \bigcirc 39 - 11$

$32 \bigcirc 28$

Step 2: Compare the expressions.

$32 \neq 28$

$f + 21 \neq 39 - f$

---

1. $(10 + 4) - 2 \bigcirc f + (4 - 3)$ **2.** $(8 + 3) \div f \bigcirc (f \times 10) - 110$

Compare. Write $>$, $<$, or $=$ for each $\bigcirc$.

3. $(13 - 6) \times 5 \bigcirc 3 \times 12$ **4.** $51 + (54 \div 6) \bigcirc 66 - (54 \div 9)$

Compare the expressions. Write equal or not equal for each.

5. 72 and $(15 - 3) \times 6$ **6.** $28 - 3$ and $(11 - 5) \times 4$

_____   _____

Problem Solving

Show your work.

7. The expression $4g - 5$ represents the height of Lars. The height of David is represented by $3g + 9$. If g is 15 inches, which person is taller?

_____

Use with text pages 116–117.

Variables and Equations

Solve each equation. Check the solution.

$5r = 30$

Way 1: Use a related multiplication fact.

$5r = 30$

Think: $5 \times 6 = 30$.

So, r must be 6.

Way 2: Use a related division fact.

$5r = 30$

$5 \times r = 30$

$r = 30 \div 5$

$r = 6$

Check.

$5r = 30$

$5 \times 6 = 30$

$30 = 30$ ✓

---

1. $r + 10 = 15$

2. $z - 12 = 6$

3. $27 \div t = 9$

4. $15 = r - 9$

_____ _____ _____ _____

5. $e \times 7 = 49$

6. $6p = 18$

7. $9 = q \div 7$

8. $s - 9 = 7$

_____ _____ _____ _____

Match each equation to the words that describe it. Then solve.

9. $5g = 40$ _____

10. $g + 20 = 30$ _____

11. $12 = g - 3$ _____

12. $g \div 6 = 7$ _____

a. Twelve is a number minus 3.

b. A number divided by 6 is 7.

c. Five times a number is 40.

d. A number plus 20 is 30.

Problem Solving

Show your work.

13. David is writing a 20-chapter book. He has already written 12 chapters. Write an equation to find the number of chapters he has left to write. Then solve the equation.

_____

_____

Use with text pages 118–121.

Problem-Solving Strategy: Write an Equation

Write an equation to solve each problem.

Rusty has 6 pottery students. She gets paid $60 for the class by the school. The amount includes the student fees plus the cost to buy two packages of clay. If each student pays $8 to take the class, how much did each bag of clay cost?

Step 1: Choose a variable. Let it stand for what you need to find out.	Let m stand for the price of a bag of clay.
Step 2: Write an equation using what you know from the problem.	$\$60 = (6 \times \$8) + 2m$
Step 3: Simplify the equation.	$\$60 = \$48 + 2m$ $\$60 - \$48 = \$48 + 2m - \$48$ $\$12 = 2m$
Step 4: Solve the equation.	$\$12 = 2m$ $\$12 \div 2 = m$ $\$6 = m$
Solution: Each package of clay cost $6.	

---

1. A basketball team won 11 games, lost 4 games, and tied the rest of the games that they played. If they played a total of 18 games, how many games did they tie?

   _____

   _____

Show your work.

2. Billy has 22 guitar picks. All his guitar picks are either purple or green. He has 6 more purple picks than green ones. How many green guitar picks does Billy have?

   _____

   _____

Use with text pages 122–125.

Function Tables

Copy and complete each function table or rule.

Rule: $4t = s$

Input	Output
t	s
5	20	← 5 × 4
6	24	← 6 × 4
10	40	← 10 × 4
15	60	← 15 × 4
50	200	← 50 × 4

Rule: $a = b + 7$

	Input	Output
	a	b
1.	7	____
2.	11	____
3.	15	____

Rule: $y = x \times 3$

	Input	Output
	y	x
4.	12	____
5.	15	____
6.	____	6

Rule: $t = s - 6$

	Input	Output
	t	s
7.	2	____
8.	____	15
9.	____	24

10. **Rule:** _____

Input	Output
y	x
27	9
30	10
45	15

Problem Solving

Show your work.

11. John bought 2 hot dogs for $4. James bought 5 hot dogs for $10. Julie bought 3 hot dogs for $6. How do you find the price of *h* hot dogs?

_____

Use with text pages 126–127.

Problem-Solving Decision:
Explain Your Solution

Solve. Explain your solution.

One truck weighs 4,138 pounds. A second truck weighs 1,887 pounds more. About how much does the second truck weigh?

The second truck weighs more, so I knew that I needed to add the two amounts. The word "about" means that I need to find an estimate. First, I rounded each addend to the nearest thousand. Then I added the numbers.

4,138	rounds to	4,000
+1,887	rounds to	+2,000
		6,000

The second truck weighs about 6,000 pounds.

---

1. Sally makes $11.92 each hour at her job selling health food. She worked 1,937 hours last year. About how much did she make?

Show your work.

_____

_____

2. Mrs. Huey weighs 135 pounds. Her daughter Margaret weighs exactly one third of Mrs. Huey's weight. How much does Margaret weigh?

_____

_____

     Use with text pages 128–129.

Multiply Multiples of 10, 100, 1,000

Use basic facts and patterns to find each product.

```
Example
        2 × 60 = _____

Think:   2 × 6 = 12
         2 × 60 = 120
```

1. 3 × 8

_____

2. 3 × 80

_____

3. 3 × 800

_____

4. 4 × 3

_____

5. 4 × 30

_____

6. 4 × 300

_____

7. 6 × 4

_____

8. 6 × 40

_____

9. 6 × 400

_____

10. 6 × 4,000

_____

11. 5 × 7

_____

12. 5 × 70

_____

13. 5 × 700

_____

14. 5 × 7,000

_____

Problem Solving

15. At The Paper Shop, Molly bought a large pack of stickers. It had 8 sheets with 40 stickers on each sheet. How many stickers were in the pack?

_____

Show your work.

Use with text pages 146–147.

Estimate Products

Estimate each product by rounding factors to their greatest place value.

Example 47 × 3

47 rounds to 50

$$47 \longrightarrow 50$$
$$\times\ 3 \longrightarrow \times\ 3$$
$$\overline{150}$$

So 47 × 3 is about 150

1. 39
   × 5

2. 68
   × 2

3. 62
   × 4

4. 325
   ×   5

5. 79
   × 8

6. 167
   ×   4

7. 725
   ×   8

8. $8.29
   ×   3

9. 3,088
   ×   7

10. 4,722
    ×   6

11. 4 × 58

12. 7 × 62

13. 9 × 38

14. 8 × $42.49

15. 3 × 495

16. 6 × 678

17. 4 × 4,298

18. 9 × $39.43

Problem Solving

19. The Fall Festival was held at school in October. Last year there were 325 people at the festival. Three times as many people attended the festival this year. About how many people attended the festival this year?

Use with text pages 148–149.

Model Multiplication by One-Digit Numbers

Tell what multiplication sentence is shown by the blocks.

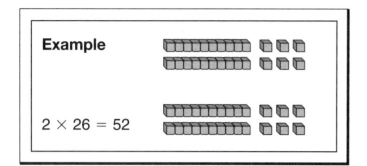

Example

2 × 26 = 52

1.

2.

3.

Use base-ten blocks to find each product.

4. 2 × 28 = ____   **5.** 5 × 13 = ____   **6.** 2 × 15 = ____   **7.** 4 × 12 = ____

8. 2 × 18 = ____   **9.** 4 × 13 = ____   **10.** 6 × 12 = ____   **11.** 3 × 24 = ____

Problem Solving

12. Tim and his 2 friends have each scored 24 points in a dart game. How many points do Tim and his friends have? Write a multiplication sentence to solve.

Show your work.

Use with text pages 150–151.

Multiply Two-Digit Numbers by One-Digit Numbers

Estimate. Then multiply.

Example 3 × 34

Think: 3 × 30 = 90

```
  1
 34
× 3
───
102
```

Remember:
• Multiply ones.
• Regroup.
• Multiply tens.

1. 22
× 4

2. 33
× 4

3. 16
× 3

4. 13
× 3

5. 24
× 3

6. 26
× 4

7. 23
× 7

8. 48
× 2

9. 44
× 3

10. 35
× 5

11. 3 × 29

12. 5 × 43

13. 4 × 28

14. 2 × 54

_____ _____ _____ _____

Problem Solving

15. Beth plans to read 28 pages each day. How many pages will she read in one week?

Show your work.

_____

Use with text pages 152–155.

Problem-Solving Strategy: Guess and Check

Use Guess and Check to solve each problem.

Yvette is thinking of two numbers. The product of the two numbers is 40. Their difference is 3. What are the two numbers Yvette is thinking of?

Think about what you know. Use the problem-solving strategy Guess and Check to find the two numbers.

Think of numbers that have a product of 40. Find the difference of the numbers.

First Number	Second Number	Product	Difference	
20	2	40	18	✗
10	4	40	6	✗
8	5	40	3	✓

The numbers Yvette is thinking of are 8 and 5.

1. Jeremy wrote down two numbers. The product of the two numbers is 12. Their difference is 4. What are the two numbers Jeremy wrote down?

   _____

   Show your work.

2. Mandy is thinking of two numbers. The product of the two numbers is 36. Their difference is 9. What are the two numbers Mandy is thinking of?

   _____

Use with text pages 156–158.

Multiply Three-Digit Numbers by One-Digit Numbers

Estimate. Then multiply.

Example 3×215

Estimate: $3 \times 200 = 600$

$$\begin{array}{r} 1 \\ 215 \\ \times\ 3 \\ \hline 645 \end{array}$$

Remember:
- Multiply the ones.
- Multiply the tens.
- Multiply the hundreds.

1. $\begin{array}{r} 427 \\ \times\ 4 \\ \hline \end{array}$

2. $\begin{array}{r} \$1.82 \\ \times\ 3 \\ \hline \end{array}$

3. $\begin{array}{r} 613 \\ \times\ 5 \\ \hline \end{array}$

4. $\begin{array}{r} 792 \\ \times\ 3 \\ \hline \end{array}$

5. $\begin{array}{r} 689 \\ \times\ 2 \\ \hline \end{array}$

6. $\begin{array}{r} \$7.18 \\ \times\ 4 \\ \hline \end{array}$

7. $\begin{array}{r} 247 \\ \times\ 6 \\ \hline \end{array}$

8. $\begin{array}{r} 818 \\ \times\ 3 \\ \hline \end{array}$

9. $\begin{array}{r} 426 \\ \times\ 4 \\ \hline \end{array}$

10. $\begin{array}{r} \$2.73 \\ \times\ 5 \\ \hline \end{array}$

11. 647×7

12. 374×8

13. 181×9

14. $\$5.71 \times 6$

_____   _____   _____   _____

_____   _____   _____   _____

Problem Solving

15. Each American flag pin sells for $2.89. A store sold 8 pins. Estimate, and then find the exact amount of sales for the flag pins.

Show your work.

_____

Use with text pages 160–163.

Multiply Greater Numbers

Multiply. Use a calculator to check.

Example

2 1
1,825
×   3
5,475

Remember:
- Multiply the ones.
- Multiply the tens.
- Multiply the hundreds.
- Multiply the thousands.

1. 2,258
×   2

2. 3,662
×   5

3. 1,452
×   3

4. $23.45
×   4

5. 3,496
×   6

6. 5,108
×   3

7. 12,042
×   2

8. 31,175
×   5

9. 1,288 × 2

10. $32.17 × 4

11. 4,234 × 5

12. 12,407 × 3

_____

_____

_____

_____

13. 5,215 × 6

14. $64.25 × 4

15. 1,759 × 8

16. $75.34 × 6

17. 11,509 × 5

_____

_____

_____

_____

_____

Problem Solving

18. Meg must pay $45.89 each month for 6 months to pay for her new guitar. How much will Meg pay for the guitar?

_____

Show your work.

Use with text pages 164–167.

Patterns With Multiples of
10, 100, 1,000

Use basic facts and patterns to find each product.

$4 \times 6 = 24$ $4 \times 60 = 240$ $40 \times 60 = 2,400$ $40 \times 600 = 24,000$ $40 \times 6,000 = 240,000$	• Multiply the non-zero digits. • Count the number of zeros in both products. • Place that many zeros behind the product of the non-zero digits.

1. 5×5 _____

5×50 _____

50×50 _____

50×500 _____

$50 \times 5,000$ _____

2. 9×4 _____

9×40 _____

90×40 _____

90×400 _____

$90 \times 4,000$ _____

3. 8×2 _____

8×20 _____

80×20 _____

80×200 _____

$80 \times 2,000$ _____

4. $\begin{array}{r} 50 \\ \times\ 6 \\ \hline \end{array}$

5. $\begin{array}{r} 80 \\ \times 80 \\ \hline \end{array}$

6. $\begin{array}{r} 700 \\ \times\ 50 \\ \hline \end{array}$

7. $\begin{array}{r} 4,000 \\ \times\quad 40 \\ \hline \end{array}$

Algebra • Inequalities Write >, <, or = for each $\bigcirc$.

8. $6 \times 40 \bigcirc 300$

9. $20 \times 90 \bigcirc 1,800$

10. $7 \times 20 \bigcirc 140$

11. $70 \times 800 \bigcirc 50,000$

Problem Solving

Show your work.

12. The school sold 200 books each day for 10 days. How many books did the school sell?

_____

43 **Use with text pages 172–173.**

Estimate Products

Estimate each product.

14 × 52	14 → 10
	×52 → ×50
	500

1.   51
    ×39

2.   2,653
    ×   69

3.   407
    × 16

4.   4,081
    ×   33

5.   397
    × 54

6.   16
    ×88

7. $9.25
    ×   48

8.   3,294
    ×   12

9. 51 × 4,639 _____

10. 6 × 34 _____

11. 42 × 748 _____

**Use mental math or estimation. Write +, −, or × for each ■.
Then use a calculator to check your work.**

12. 388 ■ 28 < 400

13. 36 ■ 100 > 3,000

Problem Solving

Show your work.

14. It takes Earth 365 days to make 1
complete trip around the sun. Estimate
the number of days it takes Earth to
travel around the sun 6 times.

_____

Use with text pages 174–175.

Model Multiplication

Use models and the Distributive Property to find each product. Show your work.

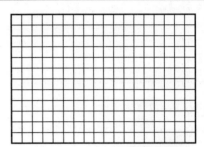

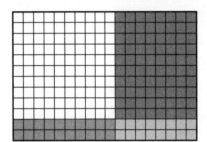

Find 12 × 18.

Step 1: Make an array with 12 rows and 18 columns.

Step 2: Break the array into hundreds, tens and ones.

Step 3: Find the partial products. Add the partial products.

$$10 \times 10 = 100$$
$$2 \times 10 = 20$$
$$8 \times 10 = 80$$
$$2 \times 8 = 16$$

$$100 + 20 + 80 + 16 = 216$$

Solution: 12 × 18 = 216

1. 13 × 14 _____

2. 11 × 15 _____

3. 19 × 16 _____

4. 12 × 23 _____

5. 25 × 18 _____

6. 21 × 13 _____

Problem Solving

7. Marcia buys one dozen eggs every time she goes to the supermarket. If she goes to the supermarket 24 times a year, how many eggs does she buy each year?

Show your work.

_____

Use with text pages 176–177.

Name _____ Date _____

Multiply 2 Two-Digit Numbers

Multiply.

15 × 13

$$
\begin{array}{r}
\overset{1}{15} \\
\times 13 \\
\hline
45 \rightarrow 3 \times 15 \\
+150 \rightarrow 10 \times 15 \\
\hline
195 \rightarrow (3 \times 15) + (10 \times 15)
\end{array}
$$

1. 76 ×51

2. 23 ×80

3. 31 ×16

4. 24 ×32

5. 45 ×37

6. 62 ×51

7. $25 × 50

8. 82 ×13

9. 73 ×35

10. 18 ×18

Use the Associative Property to multiply.

11. 15×70 _____

12. 55×90 _____

Algebra • Equations Find each value of *n*.

13. $(10 \times n) + 7 = 457$

14. $34 \times (n \times 2) = 680$

Problem Solving

15. Brennen's class is collecting food for the food drive at school. There are 26 students in his class. If each student brings in 12 cans, how many cans will the class have?

_____

Use with text pages 178–181.

Problem-Solving Decision:
Reasonable Answers

Decide whether the answer to the problem is reasonable.

Paul runs in 26-mile marathons. Last year, he ran 2 marathons. How many miles did Paul run in marathon races last year?

$$\begin{array}{r} \overset{1}{26} \\ \times\ 2 \\ \hline 52 \end{array}$$

Paul ran 52 miles in marathon races last year.

Step 1: Make sure the correct information was used.	**Step 2:** Make sure the computation is correct.	**The correct information was used and the computation is correct. The solution of 52 miles is reasonable.**

Solve. Explain why your answer is reasonable.   **Show your work.**

1. Suppose a spider can produce an egg sac that has 200 eggs each month. How many eggs could a spider lay in one year?

   _____

   _____

2. Kaylee bought an orb spider for $2.39 and a wolf spider for $3.49. She paid with a ten-dollar bill. How much change should Kaylee receive?

   _____

   _____

         Use with text pages 182–183.

Multiply Three-Digit Numbers by Two-Digit Numbers

Multiply. Estimate to make sure your answer is reasonable.

```
115 × 13

Check:   115 →  100        ¹115
         × 13 →× 10        × 13
                 1000        345
                           +1150
                            1,495
```

1.   222
      × 26

2.   304
      × 28

3.   136
      × 34

4.   316
      × 14

5.   182
      × 21

6.   409
      × 24

7. 179 × 52

8. 235 × 36

9. 501 × 15

10. 326 × 57

_____   _____   _____   _____

Mental Math Compare. Write >, <, or = for each ◯.

11. 12 × 2 × 124 ◯ 140

12. 23 + 23 + 20 ◯ 1,000 − 80

13. 63 × 9 ◯ 334 + 233

14. 758 ◯ 125 × 13

Problem Solving

15. Trey exercises for 120 minutes each day. How many minutes does he spend exercising in 2 weeks?

_____

48   **Use with text pages 184–185.**

Multiply Greater Numbers

Multiply.

```
1,523 × 21

    1
  1,523    Check:    1,523 →  1,500
 ×   21            ×   21 →×   20
   1523                    30,000
 +30460
  31,983
```

1. 1,495
   ×   19

2. 2,031
   ×   11

Estimate to check your work.

3. 2,153
   ×   14

4. 2,453
   ×   16

5. 3,463
   ×   12

6. 1,640
   ×   33

7. 4,639
   ×   62

8. 2,095
   ×   23

9. $30.47
   ×   21

Use mental math, paper and pencil, or a calculator to solve.

10. 28,765
   +13,308

11. $25.92
   ×   13

12. 47,500
   −33,200

Problem Solving

Show your work.

13. Alex ran 8 miles each day for 265
days. How many miles did Alex run?

_____

Use with text pages 186–188.

Name _____ Date _____

Model Division

Use base-ten blocks to complete the table.

	Number	Number of Equal Groups	Number in Each Group	Number Left	Number Sentence
	27	2	13	1	27 ÷ 2 = 13 R1
1.	35	6			
2.	18	5			
3.	81		9		
4.	59	7			

Problem Solving

Show your work.

5. Martin had 37 shells. He put them in 3 equal piles. How many shells were left over?

_____

50 **Use with text pages 206–207.**

Divide With Remainders

Divide. Tell if there is a remainder.

1. $6\overline{)66}$

2. $6\overline{)69}$

49 ÷ 4

$1 \times 4 = 4$ $2 \times 4 = 8$
$4 - 4 = 0$ $9 - 8 = 1$

$\begin{array}{r} 1 \\ 4\overline{)49} \\ -4\downarrow \\ \hline 09 \end{array}$ Bring down 9.

$\begin{array}{r} 12 \text{ R1} \\ 4\overline{)49} \\ -4\downarrow \\ \hline 09 \\ -8 \\ \hline 1 \end{array}$ Write the remainder.

49 ÷ 4 = 12 R1

3. $3\overline{)64}$ **4.** $4\overline{)88}$ **5.** $3\overline{)39}$ **6.** $2\overline{)82}$

7. 58 ÷ 5   **8.** 35 ÷ 3   **9.** 49 ÷ 4   **10.** 77 ÷ 7

_____   _____   _____   _____

Mental Math Write > or < for each $\bigcirc$.

11. 24 ÷ 8 $\bigcirc$ 12 ÷ 2   **12.** 44 ÷ 2 $\bigcirc$ 22 ÷ 2   **13.** 54 ÷ 6 $\bigcirc$ 72 ÷ 9

Problem Solving

Show your work.

14. Jan has 38 baseball caps. She wants to put them in groups of 3 caps each. How many groups of caps will she have? Will she have any caps left over? If so, how many?

_____

_____

_____

         Use with text pages 208–209.

Problem-Solving Application: Interpret Remainders

Solve. Explain why your answer makes sense.

A basket holds 4 dinner rolls. How many baskets are needed to hold 47 dinner rolls?

$$\begin{array}{r} 11\ R3 \\ 4\overline{)47} \\ -4 \\ \hline 07 \\ -\ 4 \\ \hline 3 \end{array}$$

How many baskets have 4 rolls? 11 baskets
How many rolls are left over? 3 rolls
Is another basket needed? yes

Another basket is needed to hold the 3 extra rolls, so 12 baskets are needed.

Solve each problem.   **Show your work.**

1. A florist received 69 roses. He wants to place the roses in buckets of water. Each bucket holds 6 roses. How many buckets will have 6 roses?

   _____

   How many roses are left over?

   _____

   How many buckets are needed for all the roses?

   _____

2. Ms. Dale bought 35 roses to give to her friends. She divided the roses equally between her 3 friends and kept the leftover roses for herself. How many roses did Ms. Dale keep?

   _____

   _____

             Use with text pages 210–213.

Regroup In Division

Divide. Check your answers.

> **Regroup the one ten left over as 10 ones.**
>
> **Check:**
>
> **13 × 3 = 39**
>
> **39 + 2 = 41**
>
> ```
>    13 R2
> 3)41
>   -3↓
>    11
>   - 9
>     2
> ```
>
> **41 ÷ 3 = 13 R2**

1. 6)60

2. 5)71

3. 38 ÷ 2   **4.** 79 ÷ 6   **5.** 95 ÷ 3   **6.** 50 ÷ 4

_____   _____   _____   _____

Algebra Functions Complete the table.

Rule: $y = x \div 4$	
x	**y**
7. 44	_____
8. 84	_____
9. _____	18
10. 24	_____

Rule: $y = x \div 8$	
x	**y**
11. 64	_____
12. _____	5
13. _____	9
14. 24	_____

Problem Solving

Show your work.

15. Three friends made 44 cupcakes. If they share the cupcakes evenly, how many cupcakes will be left over?

_____

53   **Use with text pages 214–217.**

Divide Multiples of 10, 100, and 1,000

Divide.

```
42 ÷ 6 = 7
420 ÷ 6 = 70
  ↑        ↑
1 zero   1 zero
4,200 ÷ 6 = 700
   ↑          ↑
2 zeros   2 zeros
```

1. $9 \div 3 =$ _____

$90 \div 3 =$ _____

$900 \div 3 =$ _____

$9{,}000 \div 3 =$ _____

2. $4 \div 2 =$ _____

$40 \div 2 =$ _____

$400 \div 2 =$ _____

$4{,}000 \div 2 =$ _____

3. $6 \div 1 =$ _____

$60 \div 1 =$ _____

$600 \div 1 =$ _____

$6{,}000 \div 1 =$ _____

4. $12 \div 6 =$ _____

$120 \div 6 =$ _____

$1{,}200 \div 6 =$ _____

$12{,}000 \div 6 =$ _____

5. $21 \div 7 =$ _____

$210 \div 7 =$ _____

$2{,}100 \div 7 =$ _____

$21{,}000 \div 7 =$ _____

6. $3{,}600 \div 6 =$ _____

7. $420 \div 7 =$ _____

8. $140 \div 5 =$ _____

Solve each equation.

9. $2{,}500 \div 5 = x$

10. $180 \div y = 9$

11. $1{,}600 \div n = 2$

Problem Solving

12. A giant panda bear may eat up to 420 pounds of food in a week. How many pounds of food can a panda bear eat in 1 day?

Show your work.

Use with text pages 218–219.

Estimate Quotients

Estimate. Write the basic fact you used.

154 ÷ 5
Use basic facts and
multiples of 10 to find
a new dividend.
150 ÷ 5
Think: 5 × 3 = 15
        15 × 10 = 150
150 ÷ 5 = 30
154 ÷ 5 ≈ 30

1. 4)33

2. 9)64

3. 3)26

4. 7)234

5. 204 ÷ 5

6. 26 ÷ 8

7. 195 ÷ 6

_____   _____   _____

**Decide whether the actual quotient is greater than or less than
the estimate given. Write > or < for each ◯.**

8. 27 ÷ 3 ◯ 4

9. 31 ÷ 5 ◯ 6

10. 24 ÷ 3 ◯ 7

11. 45 ÷ 9 ◯ 8

Problem Solving

Show your work.

12. Jim used 29 beads to make a necklace
for his sister. The beads he used come
in packages of 5 beads each. About
how many packages of beads did Jim
use?

_____

Use with text pages 220–223.

Three-Digit Quotients

Divide. Check your answers.

$$\begin{array}{r} 182\,\text{R1} \\ 3\overline{)547} \\ -3\downarrow \\ \hline 24 \\ -24\downarrow \\ \hline 07 \\ -6 \\ \hline 1 \end{array}$$

Remember the steps:
- Divide.
- Multiply.
- Subtract.
- Compare.
- Bring down.

1. $2\overline{)636}$

2. $4\overline{)507}$

3. $6\overline{)735}$

4. $5\overline{)319}$

5. $3\overline{)428}$

6. $3\overline{)515}$

7. $5\overline{)842}$

8. $6\overline{)815}$

9. $3\overline{)705}$

10. $8\overline{)942}$

11. $8\overline{)987}$

12. $7\overline{)945}$

13. $4\overline{)738}$

14. $6\overline{)874}$

15. $3\overline{)672}$

16. $2\overline{)735}$

Problem Solving

17. Mary has 456 baseball cards in her collection. She can fit 4 cards on a page. How many pages will she fill in her album?

_____

Use with text pages 228–229.

Name _____ Date _____

Place the First Digit of the Quotient

Divide. Check your answers.

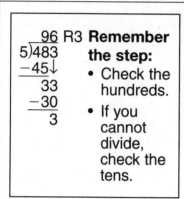

```
   96 R3  Remember
5)483     the step:
 -45↓     • Check the
   33       hundreds.
  -30     • If you
    3       cannot
            divide,
            check the
            tens.
```

1. 2)158

2. 5)375

3. 3)164

4. 9)125

5. 4)185

6. 6)560

7. 2)143

8. 6)416

9. 3)184

10. 2)179

11. 5)348

12. 4)326

13. 215 ÷ 5

14. 138 ÷ 3

15. 163 ÷ 2

16. 275 ÷ 3

_____ _____ _____ _____

Problem Solving

17. Carlos bought a large pack of 176 stickers. There are 8 sheets of stickers in the pack. How many stickers are on each sheet?

_____

57 **Use with text pages 230–233.**

Name _____ Date _____

Divide Money

Divide. Check your answers.

1. $2\overline{)\$5.12}$	**2.** $3\overline{)\$6.51}$

$$\begin{array}{r} \$2.78 \\ 3\overline{)\$8.34} \\ -6\downarrow \\ \hline 23 \\ -21\downarrow \\ \hline 24 \\ -24 \\ \hline 0 \end{array}$$

Remember the steps:
- Divide as you do with whole numbers.
- Place the dollar sign and the decimal point in the quotient.

3. $5\overline{)\$6.45}$ **4.** $3\overline{)\$5.13}$

5. $4\overline{)\$6.48}$ **6.** $7\overline{)\$9.38}$ **7.** $3\overline{)\$1.65}$ **8.** $6\overline{)\$5.88}$

9. $3\overline{)\$4.26}$ **10.** $2\overline{)\$8.24}$ **11.** $5\overline{)\$95}$ **12.** $4\overline{)\$7.24}$

13. $\$5.08 \div 4$ **14.** $\$1.83 \div 3$ **15.** $\$2.94 \div 2$ **16.** $\$5.82 \div 3$

_____   _____   _____   _____

Problem Solving

17. Ramon bought 4 glasses of lemonade for his family. He paid $3.56 for all 4 glasses. What was the price for one glass of lemonade?

_____

     Use with text pages 234–237.

Name _____ Date _____

Zeros in the Quotient

Divide. Check your answers.

```
 208 R2   Remember
3)626     the steps:
 -6 ↓     • Divide the
 026        hundreds,
 - 24       if possible.
   2      • Divide the
            tens.
          • Divide the
            ones.
```

1. 2)612

2. 5)543

3. 6)655

4. 4)816

5. 4)836

6. 7)762

7. 2)813

8. 6)485

9. 3)921

10. 2)417

11. 5)353

12. 4)419

13. $512 \div 5$

14. $735 \div 7$

15. $101 \div 2$

16. $622 \div 3$

_____   _____   _____   _____

Problem Solving

17. The sea lion show at the zoo has six shows each day. In one day, 654 people saw the sea lion show. What was the average number of people at each show?

_____

Use with text pages 238–239.

Problem-Solving Strategy:
Work Backward

Solve.

> On Friday Chris drove his car four times as far as he drove on Saturday. On
> Saturday, he drove 8 fewer miles than on Sunday. On Monday, he drove 3 more
> miles than on Sunday. Chris drove 12 miles on Monday. How many miles did
> Chris drive on Friday?
>
> **Work backward to solve.**
>
> Monday = 12 miles
>
> Sunday = 3 fewer than Monday = 12 − 3 = 9 miles
>
> Saturday = 8 fewer than Sunday = 9 − 8 = 1 mile
>
> Friday = 4 times as far as Saturday = 1 × 4 = 4 miles
>
> **Chris drove 4 miles on Friday.**

1. Julian is thinking of a number. He
subtracts 23, divides by 3, adds 4, and
multiplies by 2. The result is 14. What
is Julian's number?

    Think: What is the first operation I do
            to work backward?

_____

2. Blair bought art supplies. The paints
cost four times as much as the
brushes, which cost one-sixth of what
the canvas cost. The canvas cost $36.
How much did the paints cost?

_____

Show your work.

Use with text pages 240–243.

Name _____ Date _____

Divide Greater Numbers

Use paper and pencil or a calculator to divide.

$$\begin{array}{r} 871 \text{ R3} \\ 5\overline{)4358} \\ -40 \\ \hline 35 \\ -35 \\ \hline 08 \\ -5 \\ \hline 3 \end{array}$$

Remember the steps:
- Divide the thousands, if possible.
- Divide the hundreds.
- Divide the tens.
- Divide the ones.
- Write the remainder.

1. $2\overline{)3,463}$ 2. $5\overline{)11,243}$

3. $3\overline{)7,120}$ 4. $4\overline{)3,406}$

5. $7\overline{)6,495}$ 6. $2\overline{)5,684}$

Mental Math: Compare. Write >, <, or = for each ◯.

7. $600 \div 3 \bigcirc 800 \div 4$

8. $5,000 \div 5 \bigcirc 100 \times 8$

Algebra • Equations: Solve for *n*.

9. $n \div 9 = 600$ 10. $\$54.95 \div 5 = n$ 11. $4,836 \div n = 403$

_____   _____   _____

12. $8,000 \div 8 = n$ 13. $n \div 7 = 30$ 14. $(3,750 \div 3) - 60 = n$

_____   _____   _____

Problem Solving

Show your work.

15. Tim bought a new computer for $1,248. He paid for the computer over 6 months, making equal payments each month. How much did Tim pay each month for his computer?

_____

Use with text pages 244–247.

Factors and Multiples

Use the table on page 253.

Factors	Multiples
Factors are the shaded numbers along the top and far left of the table.	Multiples are the unshaded numbers down a column or along a row.
Example: The factors for 6 on the table are: 1, 2, 3, and 6.	Example: The first 5 multiples of 2 and 3 are: 2: 2, 4, ⑥, 8, 10 3: 3, ⑥, 9, 12, 15 6 is the common multiple of 2 and 3. Common multiples appear in both lists.

List the factors on the table for each number.

1. 18   **2.** 4   **3.** 12   **4.** 8

_____   _____   _____   _____

**Use the table to list 10 multiples for each number in each pair.
Then circle the common multiples.**

5. 2, 3   **6.** 3, 5

_____   _____

_____   _____

_____   _____

_____   _____

Problem Solving

7. Identify a number on the table that has exactly 3 factors. Write the number and list its factors.

Show your work.

_____

Use with text pages 252–253.

Prime and Composite Numbers

Prime Numbers	Composite Numbers
• one array • only 2 factors	• more than 1 array • more than 2 factors
  $1 \times 2 = 2$ → Factors: 1, 2	 $1 \times 4 = 4$ $2 \times 2 = 4$ → Factors: 1, 2, 4

In the table below, list the factors for each number. Use counters if you wish. Tell if the number is prime or composite.

	Number	Factors	Prime or Composite
1.	7		
2.	24		
3.	15		
4.	13		
5.	25		
6.	35		

Problem Solving

7. Jeff is thinking of a number between 30 and 40 that is prime. If the digits of this prime number are added together, the sum is 10. What number is Jeff thinking of?

Show your work.

_____

Use with text pages 254–257.

Problem-Solving Strategy:
Solve a Simpler Problem

Solve a simpler problem.

Valerie places twelve 5-centimeter square tiles in two rows to make a rectangle that is six tiles by two tiles. What is the distance around the rectangle they form?

Step 1: Solve a simpler problem.

Think: What would the distance around a 6 tile × 2 tile rectangle with 1-centimeter tiles be?

$6 + 2 + 6 + 2 = 16$ centimeters

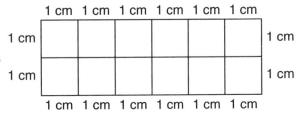

Step 2: Use this information to solve the original problem.

Think: The rectangle is 5 times as long and as wide as the diagram.
$16 × 5 = 80$

The distance around the tiles is 80 centimeters.

---

1. Rick works for a record shop. The shop is having a deal on records: Buy 3 records, get a fourth record for Free! How many records should Jan pay for if she brings 20 records up to the register?

   _____

Show your work.

2. Kelly places fifteen 2-centimeter square tiles in three rows to make a rectangle that is five tiles by three tiles. What is the distance around the rectangle they form?

   _____

Use with text pages 258–260.

Model Averages

Use counters to find the average of the numbers in each group.

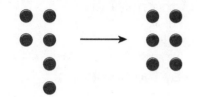

2, 4

The average of 2 and 4 is 3.

Remember:

- Show each number with a row of counters.
- Rearrange counters to have the same number in each row.
- The number in each row is the average.

1. 7, 3

_____

2. 8, 6

_____

3. 7, 9

_____

4. 4, 5, 6

_____

5. 5, 7, 9

_____

6. 9, 11, 7

_____

7. 3, 5, 8, 12

_____

8. 6, 9, 4, 5

_____

9. 3, 9, 5, 11

_____

Use counters to find the missing number in each group.

10. Average = 4
6, ▪

_____

11. Average = 7
9, ▪

_____

12. Average = 3
▪, 4

_____

Problem Solving

13. Mary's kittens weigh 4 pounds, 3 pounds, and 5 pounds. What is the average weight of Mary's kittens?

Show your work.

_____

Use with text pages 262–263.

Find Averages

Find the average of the numbers in each group.

34, 22, 37

$$\begin{array}{r} 34 \\ 22 \\ + 37 \\ \hline 93 \end{array}$$

$$\begin{array}{r} 31 \\ 3\overline{)93} \\ -9 \\ \hline 03 \\ -\ 3 \\ \hline 0 \end{array}$$

To find the average:

- Find the sum of the numbers.
- Count the addends.
- Divide the sum by the number of addends.

1. 44, 20, 35

2. 102, 388, 92

3. $15, $28, $17

_____

_____

_____

4. 6, 18, 182, 26, 13

5. 9, 4, 13, 22

6. $75, $84, $153

_____

_____

_____

Predict the average for each set of numbers. Then use a calculator to find the average.

7. 50, 100, 150, 200

8. 10, 20, 30, 40

9. 8, 8, 16, 16, 24, 24

_____

_____

_____

Problem Solving

10. It took the Smith family 3 hours to get to the state fair. They traveled 66 miles the first hour, 67 miles the second hour, and 62 miles the third hour. How many miles did they average per hour?

Show your work.

_____

Use with text pages 264–267.

Mental Math:
Divide by Multiples of 10

Use basic facts to help you divide.

20 ÷ 5 = _____
200 ÷ 50 = _____
20 ÷ 5 = 4
Think: 20 tens ÷ 5 tens = 4
20 ÷ 5 = 4
200 ÷ 50 = 4

1. 54 ÷ 6 = _____

540 ÷ 6 = _____

5,400 ÷ 6 = _____

5,400 ÷ 60 = _____

2. 28 ÷ 7 = _____

280 ÷ 7 = _____

28,000 ÷ 7 = _____

28,000 ÷ 70 = _____

3. 49 ÷ 7 = _____

4,900 ÷ 70 = _____

4. 63 ÷ 7 = _____

630 ÷ 70 = _____

5. 16 ÷ 2 = _____

16,000 ÷ 20 = _____

6. 50)‾2,500‾

7. 60)‾4,800‾

8. 90)‾360‾

9. 20)‾18,000‾

Algebra • Equations **Find each value of _n_.**

10. 4,800 ÷ n = 60

11. n ÷ 70 = 70

12. 280 ÷ 7 = n

_____

_____

_____

Problem Solving

13. Peter has 150 pieces of candy to be divided equally among 30 classmates. How many pieces of candy does each classmate get?

Show your work.

_____

Use with text pages 272–273.

Estimate Quotients

Estimate each quotient.

62 ÷ 11 = _____

Use basic facts and
multiples of 10.

62 ÷ 11
↓   ↓
60 ÷ 10 = 6

So 62 ÷ 11 = is about 6.

1. 59 ÷ 18 _____   **2.** 49 ÷ 12 _____

3. 77 ÷ 38 _____   **4.** 718 ÷ 82 _____

5. 352 ÷ 48 _____   **6.** 124 ÷ 58 _____

7. 627 ÷ 89 _____   **8.** 88 ÷ 28 _____   **9.** 248 ÷ 53 _____

10. 91)628   **11.** 18)76   **12.** 43)238   **13.** 28)243

14. 21)44   **15.** 31)179   **16.** 78)239   **17.** 92)903

Problem Solving

18. In order for the school band to get
new uniforms, they must sell at least
267 tickets to the spring concert. If
there are 34 members in the band,
about how many tickets should each
member of the band sell?

_____

               Use with text pages 274–275.

Model Division by Two-Digit Divisors

Use models to divide.

11)‾145‾

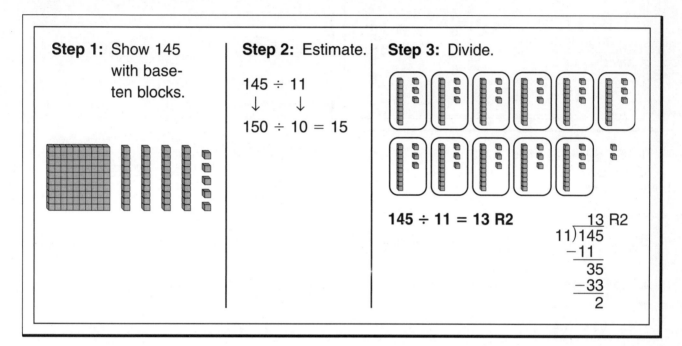

Step 1: Show 145 with base-ten blocks.

Step 2: Estimate.

145 ÷ 11
↓   ↓
150 ÷ 10 = 15

Step 3: Divide.

145 ÷ 11 = 13 R2

```
        13 R2
11)145
   −11
    35
   −33
     2
```

---

1. 36)‾79‾   **2.** 27)‾86‾   **3.** 12)‾52‾   **4.** 24)‾148‾

5. 28)‾145‾   **6.** 65)‾133‾   **7.** 29)‾175‾   **8.** 62)‾189‾

Problem Solving

9. Perry has to type 192 pages. He can type 12 pages in one day. How many days will it take him to type all 192 pages?

_____

69   **Use with text pages 276–279.**

One-Digit Quotients

Divide. Check your answer.

$43\overline{)178}$

There are not enough tens, so divide ones.

$$\begin{array}{r} 4\ R6 \\ 43\overline{)178} \\ -172 \\ \hline 6 \end{array}$$

Check:
$$\begin{array}{r} 43 \\ \times\ \ 4 \\ \hline 172 \\ +\ \ 6 \\ \hline 178 \end{array}$$

178 ÷ 43 = 4 R6

1. $23\overline{)47}$

2. $11\overline{)56}$

3. $15\overline{)80}$

4. $20\overline{)74}$

5. $31\overline{)93}$

6. $42\overline{)87}$

7. $21\overline{)75}$

8. $12\overline{)60}$

9. 251 ÷ 41

10. 724 ÷ 81

11. 216 ÷ 29

12. 129 ÷ 42

_____ _____ _____ _____

Algebra • Expressions   Compare.
Use >, <, or = for each $\bigcirc$.

13. 100 ÷ 20 $\bigcirc$ 25 ÷ 5

14. 923 ÷ 42 $\bigcirc$ 926 ÷ 42

15. 280 ÷ 7 $\bigcirc$ 2,800 ÷ 80

16. 240 ÷ 60 $\bigcirc$ 320 ÷ 80

Problem Solving

17. The stock employee at *Connie's Shoes* has 198 tennis shoes to put on display. If he puts 22 shoes on a shelf, how many shelves will he need to display the shoes?

Show your work.

_____

Use with text pages 280–281.

Two-Digit Quotients

Divide. Check your answer.

$23\overline{)488}$

There are not
enough hundreds,
so divide tens.

$488 \div 23 = 21$ R5

$$\begin{array}{r} 21 \text{ R5} \\ 23\overline{)488} \\ -46 \\ \hline 28 \\ -23 \\ \hline 5 \end{array}$$

Check:
$$\begin{array}{r} 23 \\ \times\ 21 \\ \hline 483 \\ +\ \ 5 \\ \hline 488 \end{array}$$

1. $27\overline{)804}$

2. $14\overline{)379}$

3. $36\overline{)1,574}$

4. $54\overline{)4,219}$

5. $42\overline{)765}$

6. $45\overline{)648}$

7. $949 \div 52$

8. $728 \div 47$

9. $1,421 \div 43$

10. $7,245 \div 83$

_____   _____   _____   _____

Problem Solving

11. The students at Jones Elementary
School collected 2,664 canned goods
for the food drive. They packed 36
cans in each box. How many boxes did
they use?

_____

Use with text pages 282–284.

Adjust the Quotient

Estimate. Then divide.

1. $44\overline{)489}$ **2.** $15\overline{)590}$

$46\overline{)419}$

Estimate:
$419 \div 46$

$\begin{array}{r} 9\ R5 \\ 46\overline{)419} \\ -414 \\ \hline 5 \end{array}$

$\downarrow \quad \downarrow$
$400 \div 50 = 8$

$419 \div 46 = 9\ R5$

The estimate is too small.
A better estimate is 9.

3. $46\overline{)689}$ **4.** $12\overline{)643}$

5. $44\overline{)586}$ **6.** $39\overline{)164}$

7. $322 \div 58$ **8.** $186 \div 29$ **9.** $913 \div 26$ **10.** $392 \div 33$

_____   _____   _____   _____

Problem Solving

11. Randy is installing pipes that are
11 feet long. He has to lay 363 feet of
pipe. He estimates that he will need
33 pipes. Is he right? Why or why not?

_____

_____

72   **Use with text pages 286–287.**

Focus on Problem Solving
Multistep Problems

Solve each problem.

There are 8 slices in a pizza. How many pizzas will be needed to feed 32 people if each person has 2 slices of pizza?

Step 1: Find the total number of slices of pizza needed to feed 32 people.

$$32 \times 2 = 64$$

Step 2: Find the number of pizzas needed to feed 32 people.

$$64 \div 8 = 8$$

Eight pizzas are needed to feed 32 people.

---

1. Damaris collected 98 cans and 42 bottles. She received 5 cents for each can or bottle. What operations do you need to use? How many cans and bottles did she collect? How much money did she receive?

Show your work.

_____

_____

_____

2. Lisa's dad bought 10 dozen potatoes. The potatoes were equally divided among 20 bags. How many potatoes were in each bag?

_____

Use with text pages 288–289.

Explore Customary Units of Length

Measure to the nearest inch, half inch, and quarter inch.

Use a ruler to measure the length.

0   1   2
inches

Nearest inch: <u>2 inches</u>   **Nearest half inch:** <u>2 inches</u>

Nearest quarter inch: $1\frac{3}{4}$ inches

1.

_____

Estimate the length of each object to the nearest inch. Then measure to the nearest inch, half inch, and quarter inch.

2.

3.

_____   _____

Problem Solving

4. David measured two pencils. The first pencil measured $6\frac{1}{4}$ inches long. The second pencil measured $5\frac{1}{2}$ inches long. How long are the pencils, each measured to the nearest inch?

_____

Use with text pages 306–307.

Customary Units of Weight

Find each missing number.

8 lb = _____ oz

To change from larger
units to smaller units,
multiply by the number
of ounces in 1 pound.

8 × 16 = 128

8 lb = 128 oz

1. 18 T = _____ lb

2. 176 oz = _____ lb

3. _____ T = 6,000 lb

4. _____ oz = 8 lb

**What is the best unit to weigh these items? Write *ounce,
pound,* or *ton.***

5. a can of juice

6. a helicopter

7. a slice of cheese

_____

_____

_____

Compare. Write >, <, or = for each ◯.

8. 80 oz ◯ 6 lb

9. 40,000 lb ◯ 4 T

10. 48 oz ◯ 3 lb

Problem Solving

Show your work.

11. Lotty bought 3 pounds of cheddar
cheese and 2 pounds of Swiss cheese
for a party. How many ounces of
cheese did she buy?

_____

Use with text pages 312–314.

Problem-Solving Decision:
Too Much or Too Little
Information

**Solve. If not enough information is given, tell what information
is needed to solve the problem.**

Rachael took 24 pictures. It cost her $8 to develop the pictures. Anna took 3
times as many pictures as Rachael. How many pictures did Anna take?

What is the question?   **What do I need to know?**   **What do I know?**

• How many pictures did   • How many pictures   • Rachael took 24 pictures
  Anna take?   Rachael took   • Anna took 3 times as
                                                               many pictures

Solve the problem.   24 ← number of pictures Rachael took
                              $\times$ 3 ← 3 times as many as Rachael
                               72 ← number or pictures that Anna took

Anna took 72 pictures.

---

1. Billy recorded 6 songs for his new
   CD. Each song is about 4 minutes
   long. How much will Billy make if he
   sells 50 CDs?

   _____

   _____

Show your work.

2. Crystal is training to run a marathon.
   A marathon is about 26 miles. She
   runs 8 miles each day of the week
   except Sunday, when she runs 12
   miles. How many miles would she
   run in 4 weeks?

   _____

   _____

       Use with text pages 316–317.

Explore Metric Units of Length

Measure the length to the nearest centimeter and millimeter.

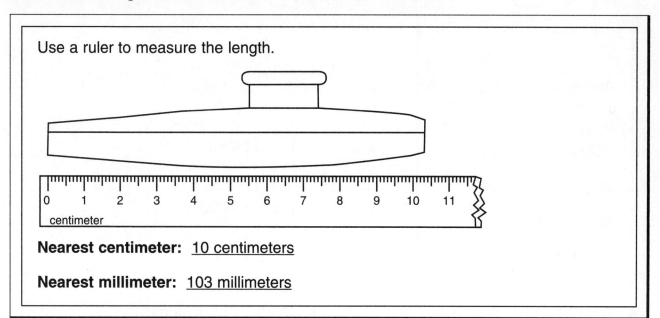

Use a ruler to measure the length.

Nearest centimeter: <u>10 centimeters</u>

Nearest millimeter: <u>103 millimeters</u>

1.

> Success is 1% inspiration
> and 99% perspiration!

_____

2.

_____

Problem Solving

Show your work.

5. Kevin measured a pencil and found that it is 148 mm long. About how many centimeters long is the pencil? Explain.

_____

_____

_____

Use with text pages 318–319.

Metric Units of Length

Find each missing number.

35 km = _____ m
To change from larger units to smaller units, multiply by the number of meters in 1 kilometer.
35 × 1,000 = 35,000
35 km = 35,000 m

1. 750 mm = _____ cm

2. 43 cm = _____ mm

3. _____ m = 600 cm

4. _____ km = 65,000 m

Choose the better estimate of length.

5. flagpole

   a. 8 m   **b.** 8 km

6. length of your thumb

   a. 5 dm   **b.** 5 cm

Copy and complete the tables. Write the rule for each table.

7.

dm	10	20	30	50	100	250
cm	100	200				

_____

8.

m	1	2	3	5	10	25
dm	10			50		

_____

Problem Solving

Show your work.

9. Freddie has a length of ribbon that is 3 meters long. If she cuts off a piece that is 242 centimeters long, how much will she have left?

_____

Use with text pages 320–321.

Name _____ Date _____

Metric Units of Capacity

Find each missing number.

┌─────────────────────────────────┐
│ **9 L = _____ mL**   │
│   │
│ To change from larger   │
│ units to smaller units,   │
│ multiply by the number   │
│ of milliliters in 1 liter.   │
│   │
│ $9 \times 1{,}000 = 9{,}000$ │
│   │
│ **9 L = 9,000 mL**   │
└─────────────────────────────────┘

1. 17,000 mL = _____ L

2. 41 L = _____ mL

3. _____ mL = 16 L

4. _____ L = 10,000 mL

Choose the better estimate of capacity of each.

5.

a. 2 mL   **b.** 2 L

6.

a. 500 mL   **b.** 50 L

7.

a. 400 mL   **b.** 4 L

**Choose the better unit to measure each capacity.
Write *milliliters* or *liters*.**

8. an eyedropper

9. a large pitcher

10. a spoon

_____   _____   _____

Problem Solving

Show your work.

11. Jessica has 12 bottles of water. Each
bottle has a capacity of 750 mL. How
many liters of water can the bottles
hold?

_____

81   **Use with text pages 322–324.**

Metric Units of Mass

Find each missing number.

13 kg = _____ g

To change from larger
units to smaller units,
multiply by the number
of grams in 1 kilogram.

13 × 1,000 = 13,000

13 kg = 13,000 g

1. 27,000 g = _____ kg

2. 200 kg = _____ g

3. _____ g = 15 kg

4. _____ kg = 8,000 g

Choose the better estimate of the mass of each.

5.

a. 800 g **b.** 800 kg

6.

a. 4 g **b.** 4 kg

7.

a. 1,000 kg **b.** 1,000 g

Compare. Write >, <, or = for each ◯.

8. 47 kg ◯ 4,700 g

9. 56,000 kg ◯ 56 g

10. 7,000 g ◯ 60 kg

Problem Solving

11. A store sold 45 kilograms of flour and
12 kilograms of sugar. How many
grams of flour and sugar did the store
sell?

Show your work.

_____

Use with text pages 326–328.

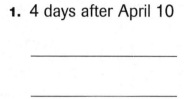
Calendar

Use the calendars on Page 334. Write the day and the date.

> **Find 3 days before May 5.**
> From May 5 move back 3 days.
> Answer: Monday, May 2

1. 4 days after April 10

_____

_____

2. 6 days before April 20

_____

3. 9 days after May 12

_____

4. 2 weeks before May 12

_____

5. 4 weeks after April 5

_____

Use the Units of Time chart on Page 334. Find each missing number.

> **3 weeks = _____ days**
> 7 days = 1 week, so 3 × 7 = 21
> 3 weeks = 21 days

6. 3 years = _____ weeks

7. 2 centuries = _____ years

8. 1 year 9 weeks = _____ weeks

9. 2 years 4 months = _____ months

Problem Solving

Show your work.

10. It takes Jenny's family 2 days to drive to the shore. They spend 8 days at the shore, then drive home again. They left their home early on Thursday, May 5. What day and date will they return home?

_____

Use with text pages 334–335.

Elapsed Time

Tell what time it will be.

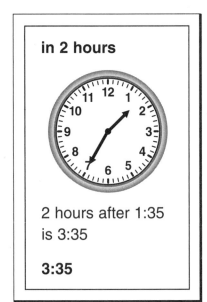

in 2 hours

2 hours after 1:35 is 3:35

3:35

1. in 35 minutes

_____

2. in 6 hours

_____

3. in 3 hours

_____

4. in 18 minutes

_____

Start: 2:15 P.M.
End: 4:00 P.M.

1 h 45 min

Look at each pair of times. Write how much time has passed.

5. Start: 3:15 A.M.
   End: 4:30 A.M.

_____

6. Start: 11:00 A.M.
   End: 1:15 P.M.

_____

7. Start: 9:05 P.M.
   End: 1:50 A.M.

_____

8. Start: 7:45 A.M.
   End: 10:00 A.M.

_____

Problem Solving

Show your work.

9. Emily catches the school bus at 7:45 A.M. She needs 30 minutes to get dressed, 15 minutes to eat breakfast, and 10 minutes to walk to the school bus. What the latest time Emily can awake in the morning to get to the bus on time?

_____

       Use with text pages 336–339.

Problem-Solving Strategy:
Guess and Check

Use Guess and Check to solve each problem.

A waiter at a restaurant collected $59 in tips. He collected only five- and one-dollar bills. He collected 15 bills in all. How many of each kind of bill did the waiter collect?

You can use Guess and Check to solve the problem.
Try two numbers. If they are not correct, use your result to improve your next guess.

Number of one-dollar bills	Number of five-dollar bills	Total	Check
5	10	$5 \times 1 = 5$ $10 \times 5 = 50$ $5 + 50 = 55$	Too low
3	12	$3 \times 1 = 3$ $12 \times 5 = 60$ $3 + 60 = 63$	Too high
4	11	$4 \times 1 = 4$ $11 \times 5 = 55$ $4 + 55 = 59$	Correct

The waiter collected 4 one-dollar bills and 11 five-dollar bills.

1. Bernadette's math test has 14 sections. Each section has either 8 or 12 problems. How many sections are there of each size if the test is 132 problems long?

_____

2. A moving truck rental company has a total of 24 trucks in its lot. The trucks are either 4-wheelers or 18-wheelers. How many of each kind of truck does the company have if the total number of wheels is 138?

_____

Use with text pages 340–342.

Name _____ Date _____

Temperature and Negative Numbers

Write each temperature.

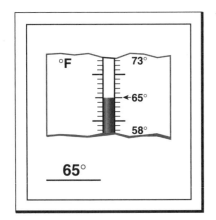

65°

1.

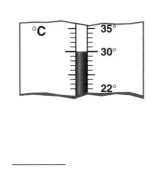

_____

2.

_____

Find the difference between the temperatures.

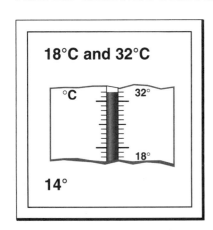

14°

3. 39°F and 75°F

_____

4. ⁻4°C and ⁻20°C

_____

5. 68°F and 92°F

_____

6. ⁻14°C and 0°C

_____

Choose the better estimate of the temperatures.

7. go skiing

   a. 32° F   **b.** 98° F

8. a glass of juice

   a. 73° C   **b.** 20° C

9. an autumn afternoon

   a. 15° F   **b.** 55° F

Problem Solving

Show your work.

10. A cold front was coming through Baytown. At 9:00 A.M., the temperature was 37°F. The temperature dropped an average of 5 degrees per hour over the next 6 hours. What was the temperature at 3:00 P.M.?

_____

86   **Use with text pages 344–347.**

Problem-Solving Application:
Use Temperature

Solve.

> The temperature was 43°F in the morning. It rose 26 degrees during the day and then dropped 17 degrees by 10:00 P.M. What was the temperature at 10:00 P.M.?
>
> **Step 1:** Start at 43° F.
>
> **Step 2:** Add 26°.
>
> $$43 + 26 = 69°$$
>
> **Step 3:** Subtract 17°.
>
> $$69 - 17 = 52°$$
>
> **At 10:00 P.M. the temperature was 52°.**

1. On Thursday, the high temperature was 23°C and the low temperature was 14°C. On Sunday, the high temperature was 18°C and the low temperature was 10°C. What is the difference in Thursday's temperatures? What is the difference in Sunday's temperatures? Which day had the greatest difference in temperatures?

Show your work.

_____

2. A thermometer shows 35°F. The wind makes the air feel 17 degrees colder. How cold does it feel?

_____

Use with text pages 348–350.

Collect and Organize Data

Use the list to make a tally chart on a separate sheet of paper.
Then use the tally chart for problems 1–6. For questions 4–5,
write *true* or *false* for each statement.

Student	Favorite Color	Student	Favorite Color	Student	Favorite Color
Dennis	Yellow	Rachael	Red	Missy	Red
Jessy	Green	Ryan	Blue	Ralph	Yellow
Joe	Yellow	Kelly	Green	Helen	Red
Matt	Blue	Hector	Yellow	Itto	Red
Monica	Yellow	Georgia	Yellow	Rusty	Blue
Arnold	Blue	Karen	Green	Laura	Red
Terri	Yellow	Lucy	Yellow	Jason	Red
Mary	Red	Harold	Green	Nathan	Blue

How many students chose red?

Count the tallies for red. Remember
that a ✝✝✝✝ stands for 5.

Seven students chose red.

1. Which answer was given the most
   often? least often?

   _____

2. How many classmates answered the
   survey question?

   _____

3. What is the order of colors from least
   popular to most popular?

   _____

4. Half of the people surveyed choose
   either red or blue.

   _____

5. More people chose yellow than green
   and blue combined.

   _____

Problem Solving

Show your work.

6. Kerry says that one-third of the
   classmates surveyed chose yellow. Is
   she correct? Explain how you know.

   _____

   _____

88 **Use with text pages 356–358.**

Problem-Solving Strategy:
Make a Table

Make a table to solve each problem.

Daisy is 16 years old. Mom is 37 years old. How old will they both be when Mom is twice as old as Daisy?

Divide Mom's age by Daisy's age until you get a quotient of 2.

Mom's Age	Daisy's Age	Quotient
37	16	37 ÷ 16 = 2 R5
38	17	38 ÷ 17 = 2 R4
39	18	39 ÷ 18 = 2 R3
40	19	40 ÷ 19 = 2 R2
41	20	41 ÷ 20 = 2 R1
42	21	42 ÷ 21 = 2

Mom will be twice as old as Daisy when Mom is 42 years old and Daisy is 21 years old.

1. Kate is 4 years older than Margaret. In 7 years, the sum of their ages will be 70. How old are they now? How do you find Kate's age using Margaret's?

_____

Show your work.

2. Sally's grandfather is 67 years old. Sally is 19 years old. At what age will Sally be exactly one third of her grandfather's age? How old will her grandfather be then?

_____

Use with text pages 360–362.

Mean, Median, Mode, and Range

Find the mean, median, mode, and range of each set of data.

42, 13, 51, 51, 67, 62, 36 $42 + 13 + 51 + 51 + 67 + 62 + 36 = 322$ $322 \div 7 = 46$ **The mean of the data is 46.**	13, 36, 42, 51, 51, 62, 67 The middle value is 51. **The median of the data is 51.**
13, 36, 42, 51, 51, 62, 67 The value that occurs the most is 51. **The mode of the data is 51.**	$67 - 13 = 54$ **The range of the data is 54.**

1. 34, 41, 37, 29, 33, 35, 43

_____

_____

_____

_____

2. 9, 22, 93, 31, 35, 37, 38, 31

_____

_____

_____

_____

3. 24, 20, 24, 12, 60, 10

_____

_____

_____

4. 73, 92, 67, 45, 86, 69, 81, 70, 65

_____

_____

_____

Problem Solving

Show your work.

5. Mary collected 31 rocks on Monday, 27 on Tuesday, 27 on Wednesday, 33 on Thursday, and 22 on Friday. What is the mean number of rocks she collected?

_____

Use with text pages 364–365.

Line Plots

Use the line plot to answer each question.

What is the median of the data?

Order the data from least to greatest and find
the middle value.

0, 1, 1, 1, 1, 1, 2, 2, 2, **2**, 2, 2, 2, 3, 3, 3, 3, 3, 4

The median of the data is 2.

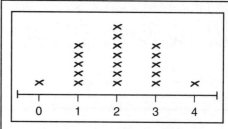

**Hours of Video Game Playing by
Fourth Grade Students on Saturday**

1. According to the line plot, how many students were
   surveyed?

   _____

2. What is the range of the data?

   _____

3. What is the mean of the data?

   _____

4. What is the mode of the data?

   _____

Problem Solving

Show your work.

5. Suppose that 5 more students had
   played 2 hours of video games on
   Saturday. What would the mean of the
   data set be then? Explain how you
   found your answer.

_____

Use with text pages 366–367.

Stem-and-Leaf Plots

What is the median of the data?

Find the middle value on the plot.

The median of the data is 37.

Stem	Leaves
1	2 5 8
2	3 3
3	6 7
4	0
5	1 2 3 3 5

The table shows how much Michael made each week by mowing lawns.

1. Make a stem-and-leaf plot of the amount earned.

2. How many leaves are in the stem-and-leaf plot? What do they represent?

   _____

   _____

   _____

Week	Amount Earned
1	$37
2	$58
3	$55
4	$61
5	$58
6	$64
7	$67
8	$61
9	$58

3. What was the greatest amount money that Mark earned in one week? the least?

   _____

   _____

4. What is the median weekly amount?

   _____

5. What weekly amount did Mark earn most often?

   _____

Use with text pages 368–370.

Double Bar Graphs

During which month did Raleigh have more rainy days than Cleveland?

Compare the bar for Raleigh and the bar for Cleveland during each month.

In July, there were 10 rainy days in Cleveland and 11 rainy days in Raleigh.

During the month of July, Raleigh had more rainy days than Cleveland.

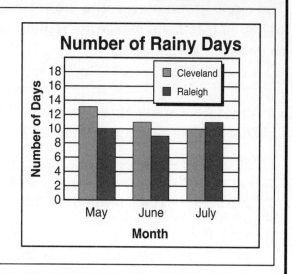

Jessie made a table to show the scores for his team, the Goldenrods, and the opposing team in the first three games of the season. Use the table to make a double bar graph. Use the graph to answer each question.

Points Scored in Each Game			
Team	Game 1	Game 2	Game 3
Goldenrods	47	51	63
Opponents	42	55	57

1. What interval did you choose for your graph? Explain your choice.

   _____

Problem Solving

2. During which game did the opponents score more points than the Goldenrods? Explain how you found your answer.

   _____

   _____

93   **Use with text pages 376–377.**

Circle Graphs

The circle graph represents the results of Alexander's survey of his 20 classmates' favorite restaurants. Use the circle graph to answer each question.

About how many students named _Kyler's Thai_ as their favorite restaurant?

Kyler's Thai is represented by $\frac{1}{4}$ of the graph. This means that $\frac{1}{4}$ of the 20 students named _Kyler's Thai_ as their favorite restaurant.

$20 \div 4 = 5$

About 5 students named _Kyler's Thai_ as their favorite restaurant.

Favorite Restaurants

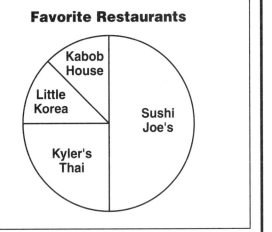

Use the circle graph above for Problems 1–3.

1. About what fraction of the students chose Kabob House?

   _____

2. About how many students named Sushi Joe's as their favorite restaurant?

   _____

Problem Solving

3. Did more students choose _Little Korea_ or _Kyler's Thai_? Explain how you found your answer.

   _____

   _____

   _____

94 **Use with text pages 378–379.**

Problem-Solving Application:
Interpret a Line Graph

Use the line graph to answer each question.

Between which two consecutive points did the greatest change occur?

Compare the distance between each pair of consecutive points. The distance between point A and point B is greater than the distance between any other two consecutive points.

The greatest change occurred between points A and B.

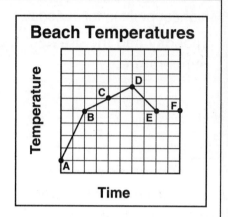

Beach Temperatures

1. Was it colder at the start of the day or at the end of the day? Explain how you found your answer.

   _____

   _____

2. At what point did the temperature stop rising? Explain how you found your answer.

   _____

   _____

3. Between which two consecutive points did the least change occur? Explain how you found your answer.

   _____

   _____

Use with text pages 380–381.

Name _____ Date _____

Read and Make Line Graphs

Which day had the greatest high temperature?

Look for the highest point on the graph. The highest point is for Tuesday.

Tuesday had the greatest high temperature.

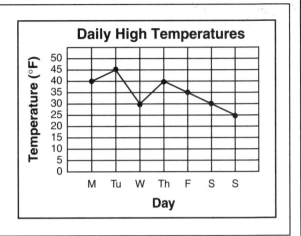

Use the table below to make a line graph. Use the line graph to answer each question.

Plant Growth	
Week	**Height**
1	1 inch
2	4 inches
3	6 inches
4	11 inches
5	14 inches

1. How tall was the plant at 3 weeks?

   _____

2. During which 2 consecutive weeks did the plant grow the most?

   _____

Problem Solving

3. Would you expect the plant's height to be 10 inches, 16 inches, or 30 inches at week 6? Explain your reasoning.

   _____

 Use with text pages 382–383.

Analyze Graphs

**Choose a graph to display each set of data. Write *bar graph,
circle graph, line graph,* or *pictograph.* Explain your choice.**

> **the high temperatures in Burlington,
> Vermont from Monday to Sunday**
>
> A **line graph** is a good choice to show
> change over time, such as temperature.

1. the results of a survey of students' favorite snacks

_____

_____

2. how much money a business earned over time

_____

_____

3. a comparison of the heights of different students

_____

_____

Problem Solving

4. When is a bar graph a better choice than a pictograph?
Explain your reasoning.

_____

_____

97 **Use with text pages 384–386.**

Points, Lines, and Line Segments

Use words and symbols to name each figure.

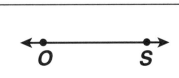

The figure is a line with points *O* and *S*.

⟷

line *OS*, *OS*

1.

_____

2.

_____

3.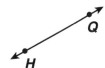

_____

Write *parallel*, *intersecting*, or *perpendicular* to best describe the relationship between each pair of lines.

4.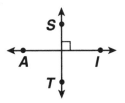

_____

5.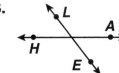

_____

6.

_____

7.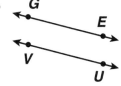

_____

Problem Solving

8. Draw an example of two parallel lines that are crossed by one perpendicular line.

Use with text pages 404–406.

Rays and Angles

Name each angle in three ways. Then classify the angle as
acute, *obtuse*, *right*, or *straight*.

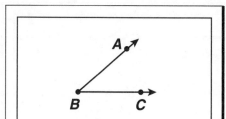

∠ B, ∠ ABC,
∠ CBA
The angle is acute.

1. X
   Y   Z

_____

_____

_____

_____

2. R
   S   T

_____

_____

_____

_____

3. M   O
      N

_____

_____

_____

_____

4. G
   F
   E

_____

_____

_____

_____

5. D
   B   C

_____

_____

_____

_____

6. R   T
   S

_____

_____

_____

_____

7. W
   X   Y

_____

_____

_____

_____

Problem Solving

8. Merideth and Luis both started at the same spot. They
   walked away from each other in opposite directions. They
   stayed on the same line. What angle did their paths form?
   Explain how you know.

_____

_____

_____

Use with text pages 408–409.

Measure Angles

Use a protractor to draw an angle having each measure. Then
classify the angle as *right, acute, obtuse,* or *straight*.

60°

Draw a ray. Align the 0°
mark with the ray. Draw a
ray from the vertex through
the point for 60°.

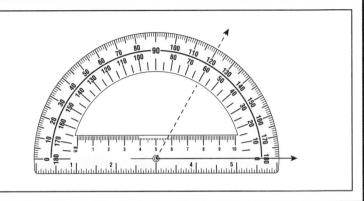

1. 50°　　　　　　　　**2.** 90°　　　　　　　　**3.** 20°

_____　　　　_____　　　　_____

4. 70°　　　　　　　　**5.** 180°　　　　　　　**6.** 130°

_____　　　　_____　　　　_____

Problem Solving

7. Is it possible to draw a straight angle accurately using a ruler
instead of a protractor? Explain your answer.

_____

_____

_____

_____

　　　100　　　**Use with text pages 410–411.**

Quadrilaterals and Other Polygons

Name each polygon. If the polygon is a quadrilateral, write all names that apply.

The polygon is a quadrilateral.
It has opposite sides parallel and four sides the same length.
It is a parallelogram and a rhombus.

1.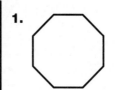

_____

_____

2.

_____

_____

3.

_____

_____

Tell if each figure is a polygon or not. For a polygon, tell if it appears to be regular or irregular.

4.

_____

_____

5.

_____

_____

6.

_____

_____

7.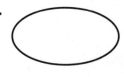

_____

_____

Problem Solving

8. Megan drew a shape with four sides. Two of the sides were parallel. The other two sides were not parallel. What kind of shape did Megan draw?

_____

101 **Use with text pages 412–414.**

Classify Triangles

Classify each triangle as *equilateral*, *isosceles*, or *scalene* and as *right*, *obtuse*, or *acute*.

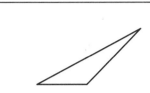

The triangle has 3 sides of unequal length.
It is scalene.
The triangle has 1 obtuse angle.
It is obtuse.

1.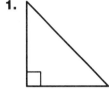

_____

_____

2.

_____

_____

3.

_____

_____

Draw one example of each triangle described below.

4. an isosceles triangle that is also a right triangle

5. an equilateral triangle that is also an acute triangle

6. a scalene triangle that is also an obtuse triangle

Problem Solving

7. Misty drew a triangle. One angle is 120°. Two of the sides measure 5 cm and 8 cm in length. The sum of the lengths of all three sides is 21 cm. What kind of triangle did Misty draw?

_____

Use with text pages 416–417.

Problem-Solving Strategy:
Find a Pattern

Find the pattern to solve each problem.

A border has a repeating design that shows a star, a circle, and a square in a row. The circle is just after the star. The square is first. Which figure is eighth in the pattern?

Use the clues to make the pattern.

Think: The square is first. The circle comes after the star, so the star must be second.

Draw the pattern. Repeat the pattern.

☐ ☆ ○ ☐ ☆ ○ ☐ ☆ ○

Find the eighth figure.

The star is eighth in the pattern.

---

1. Matthew made the pattern below. Describe the pattern.
   What would the next two letters in the pattern be?

   A Z U Z A Z U Z _____ _____

   _____

   _____

2. Judith made the design below. Describe the pattern.
   What figures will complete the pattern?

   ♦ ♠ ♠ ♥ ♦ _____ ♠ ♥ _____ ♠ ♠ ♥

   _____

   _____

103   **Use with text pages 418–420.**

Circles

Name the part of each circle that is shown with a point or a point and a dashed line. Write *center, radius, diameter,* or *chord*.

The line segment has its endpoints on the circle. It does not pass through the center.
It is a chord.

1.

_____

2.

_____

3.

_____

For exercises 4–5, trace around a circular object. Draw the part or parts of the circle described.

4. a set of two diameters that are perpendicular to each other

5. three chords which form a triangle

Problem Solving

6. The hour hand on a clock starts on the 12:00 noon. George checks the clock later in the day. The hour hand has made a three-quarter turn around the clock. What time is it?

_____

Use with text pages 422–424.

Congruent Figures

Do the figures in each pair appear to be congruent?
Write *yes* or *no*.

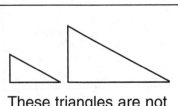

These triangles are not
the same size.

No, they are not
congruent.

1.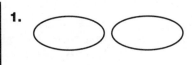

_____

2.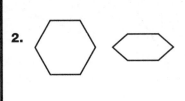

_____

Draw a figure congruent to each figure shown.

3. _____

4. _____

Use the figures at the right for Problem 5.

5. Use a centimeter ruler. Are the two
figures congruent rectangles?

_____

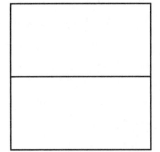

Problem Solving

6. Use the grid paper to draw a square.
Draw lines that connect the opposite
corners using a ruler. Are the resulting
triangles congruent?

_____

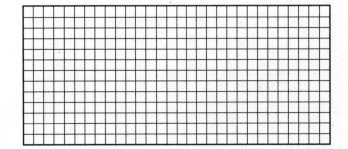

105 **Use with text pages 430–432.**

Rotations, Reflections, and Translations

**Tell how each figure was moved. Write *rotation, reflection,*
or *translation.***

The figure was flipped
over a line.

This shows a
reflection.

1.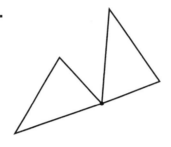

_____

2.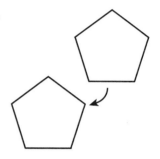

_____

**Trace the figure at the right and cut it out. Use the tracing
for Problem 3.**

3. Lucy rotated this figure 90° to the left.
What does the figure look like now?
Draw a picture to show your answer.

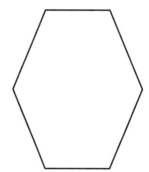

Problem Solving

4. Suppose that the upper-case letter T
was flipped over a vertical line and
then rotated 180° to the right. What
would it look like? Draw a picture of
the letter.

Use with text pages 434–435.

Problem-Solving Strategy:
Act It Out

Solve each problem.

Can these five figures be arranged to form a figure that is congruent to the large triangle at the right?

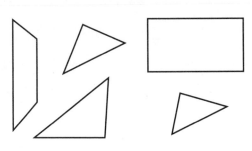 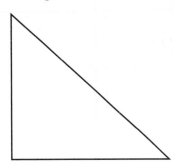

You can make models and Act it Out to solve the problem. Trace the 5 figures and cut them out. Try to make the large triangle.

The figures can be arranged to form a figure that is congruent to the large triangle at the right.

---

1. Use two of the figures above to form a figure congruent to the triangle shown below. Make a drawing to show your work.

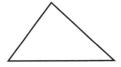

2. Can 5 toothpicks be used to form 2 congruent triangles? Make a drawing to show your answer.

         Use with text pages 436–438.

Symmetry

Is the dashed line a line of symmetry? Write _yes_ or _no_.

If you fold the figure along the dashed line, the two parts match exactly.

Yes, the dashed line is a line of symmetry.

1.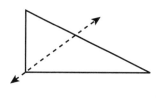

_____

2.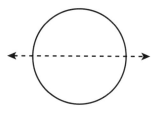

_____

How many lines of symmetry does the figure have?

3.

_____

4. K

_____

5.

_____

6. 8

_____

Trace each figure. Does the figure have rotational symmetry? Write _yes_ or _no_.

7.

_____

8.

_____

9.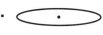

_____

Problem Solving

10. How many upper case letters in the alphabet have 2 or more lines of symmetry? List each letter.

_____

Use with text pages 440–442.

Problem-Solving Application:
Visual Thinking

Use visual thinking to solve each problem.

What would the box look like if it was turned on its right side?

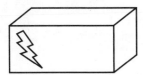

Use visual thinking to decide what the box would look like if it was turned on its right side.

If the box was turned on its right side, it would look like this.

1. What would the box look like if it was turned on its left side? Draw it. Use the original box.

2. What will be the next figure in this pattern? Draw it.

Use with text pages 444–446.

Explore Perimeter and Area

Solve.

> Do the rectangles have the same perimeter?
> Do the rectangles have the same area?
>
> 5 units
> 2 units
> 4 units
> 3 units
>
> Find the perimeter and area of each rectangle.
>
> | Length | Width | Perimeter | Area |
> |--------|-------|-----------|------|
> | 5 units | 2 units | 14 units | 10 square units |
> | 4 units | 3 units | 14 units | 12 square units |
>
> **The rectangles have the same perimeter.**
> **The rectangles do not have the same area.**

1. Draw two rectangles with the same
area but with different perimeters.

2. Draw two rectangles with different
areas but the same perimeter.

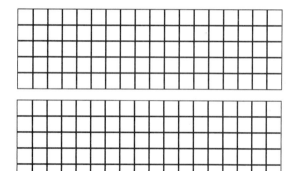

Problem Solving

3. Draw a rectangle with an area of 24
square units and a perimeter greater
than 24 units.

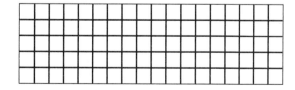

110   **Use with text pages 452–453.**

Perimeter

Find the perimeter of each polygon.

14 in.

3 in.

You can add the side lengths.

$P = 3 + 14 + 3 + 14$

P = 34 in.

You can use a formula.

$P = (2 \times l) + (2 \times w)$

$P = (2 \times 3) + (2 \times 14)$

$P = 6 + 28$

P = 34 in.

Find the perimeter of each polygon.

1.

16 cm

2.

12 in.

7 in.

3.
15 ft

_____

_____

_____

Write a formula to find each perimeter. Then solve.

4.
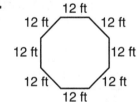
12 ft
12 ft   12 ft
12 ft   12 ft
12 ft   12 ft
12 ft

5.
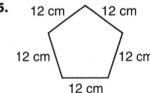
12 cm   12 cm
12 cm   12 cm
12 cm

6.
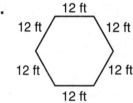
12 ft
12 ft   12 ft
12 ft   12 ft
12 ft

_____

_____

_____

Problem Solving

7. A rectangular room is 6 yards long and 12 feet wide. Find the perimeter in feet. Then find the perimeter in yards.

Show your work.

_____

Use with text pages 454–455.

Area

Find the area of each figure.

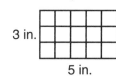

You can draw a model and count the squares.

3 in.

5 in.

A = 15 square feet
A = 15 ft²

You can use a formula.

A = length × width

$A = l × w$
$A = 5 × 3$
A = **15 square feet**
A= **15 ft²**

1.

13 in.

4 in.

_____

2.

15 ft

7 ft

_____

3.

20 cm

8 cm

_____

Find the perimeter and area for each rectangle.

4. 9 yd long, 11 yd wide

_____

_____

5. 14 ft long, 9 ft wide

_____

_____

6. 18 cm long, 6 cm wide

_____

_____

Problem Solving

7. Helen wants to carpet her bedroom. Her bedroom is 14 feet long and 12 feet wide. How many square feet of carpeting will Helen need to carpet the entire bedroom?

_____

Show your work.

Use with text pages 456–458.

Name _____ Date _____

Perimeter and Area of Complex Figures

Find the area of the figure.

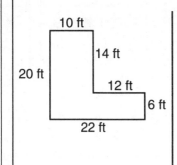

Step 1: Separate the figure into 2 rectangles.

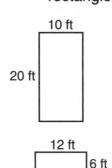

Step 2: Use a formula to find the area of each rectangle.

$A = l \times w$
$A = 20 \times 10$
$A = 200$

$A = l \times w$
$A = 12 \times 6$
$A = 72$

Step 3: Add both areas to find the area of the whole figure.

$A = 200 + 72$
$A = 272$

The area of the figure is 272 ft².

Find the perimeter and the area of each figure.

1.

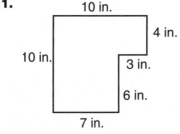

2.

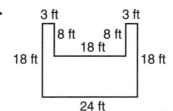

3.

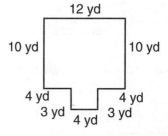

_____

_____

Problem Solving

4. Hugo wants to carpet the room below. If carpet costs $2 per square foot, how much will it cost to carpet the room?

Show your work.

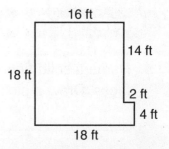

_____

113

Use with text pages 460–462.

Solid Figures and Nets

Name the solid figure each object looks like.

The figure has no faces. It is not made up of polygons.

It is a sphere.

1.

_____

2.

Crackers

_____

Name the solid figure that can be made with each net.

3.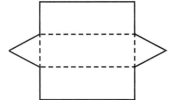

_____

4.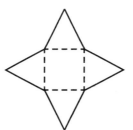

_____

5.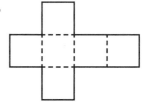

_____

Complete the table.

	Solid Figure	Number of Faces	Number of Edges	Number of Vertices
6.	Cone			
7.	Triangular Pyramid			
8.	Square Pyramid			

Problem Solving

9. Name a solid figure that has only 2 faces. Draw a picture of it.

Show your work.

_____

Use with text pages 464–466.

Name _____ Date _____

Volume

Find the volume of each figure.

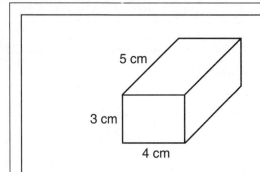

You can use a formula.

$V = $ length $\times$ width $\times$ height

$V = l \times w \times h$
$V = 5 \times 4 \times 3$
$V = 60$ cubic cm
$V = 60$ cm^3

1.

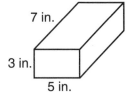

7 in.
3 in.
5 in.

_____

2.

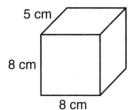

5 cm
8 cm
8 cm

_____

3.

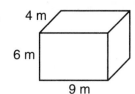

4 m
6 m
9 m

_____

4.

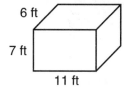

6 ft
7 ft
11 ft

_____

5.

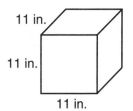

11 in.
11 in.
11 in.

_____

6.

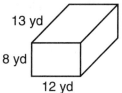

13 yd
8 yd
12 yd

_____

7.

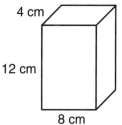

4 cm
12 cm
8 cm

_____

8.

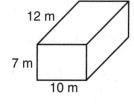

12 m
7 m
10 m

_____

Problem Solving

9. The volume of a package is 96 cubic inches. The height of the package is 4 inches. The length of the package is 6 inches. What is the width of the package? Explain how you found your answer.

Show your work.

_____

115   **Use with text pages 468–469.**

Problem-Solving Application: Use Formulas

Use a formula to solve.

Lars has a storage trunk that is 4 feet long, 2 feet high, and 3 feet wide. He wants to paint a border around the edges of the front panel of the trunk. How long will the border be?

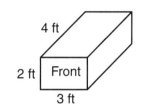

Find the perimeter of the front panel. Use the formula for perimeter of a rectangle.

$P = (2 \times l) + (2 \times w)$
$P = (2 \times 2) + (2 \times 3)$
$P = 4 + 6$
$P = 10$ ft

The border will be 10 feet long.

Choose a closet in your house.

Show your work.

1. What are the dimensions of the closet?

   (**Hint:** Make sure you measure in the same units.)

   _____

   _____

2. What is the area of the floor of the closet? How much space is in the closet? How many square feet of wallpaper would you need to cover the back and sides of the closet?

   _____

   _____

 Use with text pages 470–472.

Find Part of a Number

Find the fractional part of each number.

$\frac{2}{3}$ **of 12**

Divide to find the number in each group.

$12 \div 3 = 4$

Multiply by the number of groups.

$4 \times 2 = 8$

$\frac{2}{3}$ **of 12 = 8**

1. $\frac{2}{3}$ of 6   **2.** $\frac{3}{8}$ of 24

_____   _____

3. $\frac{2}{5}$ of 25   **4.** $\frac{3}{10}$ of 50

_____   _____

5. $\frac{4}{7}$ of 35   **6.** $\frac{3}{4}$ of 36   **7.** $\frac{1}{4}$ of 32   **8.** $\frac{2}{11}$ of 44

_____   _____   _____   _____

9. $\frac{3}{5}$ of 45   **10.** $\frac{5}{9}$ of 27   **11.** $\frac{5}{8}$ of 64   **12.** $\frac{7}{10}$ of 80

_____   _____   _____   _____

13. $\frac{11}{15}$ of 45   **14.** $\frac{3}{20}$ of 120   **15.** $\frac{2}{3}$ of 42   **16.** $\frac{1}{8}$ of 40

_____   _____   _____   _____

Problem Solving

Show your work.

17. Blake has 15 musical instruments. Guitars make up $\frac{2}{5}$ of the instruments Blake has. How many of the musical instruments are guitars?

_____

Use with text pages 502–503.

Problem-Solving Strategy: Draw a Picture

Draw a picture to solve each problem.

Kacey painted several pieces of pottery. One third of the pieces were plates, $\frac{1}{6}$ of the pieces were bowls, and 10 of the pieces were cups. How many pieces of pottery did Kacey paint?

$\frac{1}{3} = \frac{2}{6}; \frac{2}{6}$ of the pieces were plates

$\frac{2}{6} + \frac{1}{6} = \frac{3}{6}; \frac{3}{6}$ of the pieces were plates or bowls

$\frac{6}{6} - \frac{3}{6} = \frac{3}{6}; \frac{3}{6}$ of the pieces were cups

Draw a picture using what you know.

$\frac{3}{6} = \frac{1}{2}$

Cups make up half of the total pieces painted.

$\frac{1}{2}$ of the total pieces painted $= 10$

1					
$\frac{1}{6}$	$\frac{1}{6}$	$\frac{1}{6}$	$\frac{1}{6}$	$\frac{1}{6}$	$\frac{1}{6}$
plates		bowls		cups	

Kacey painted 20 pieces of pottery.

Problem Solving

1. Beth spent $\frac{3}{8}$ of her money on guitar strings, $\frac{1}{8}$ of her money on guitar picks, and $15 on a guitar tuner. How much money did Beth have before buying guitar accessories?

Show your work.

_____

2. Rusty arranged ornaments by color. One fourth of the ornaments were green, $\frac{7}{20}$ of the ornaments were yellow, and 24 of the ornaments were red. How many ornaments did Rusty arrange?

_____

Use with text pages 504–507.

Mixed Numbers and Improper Fractions

Write an improper fraction for the shaded parts. Then write each as a mixed number or as a whole number.

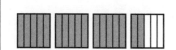

There are 3 whole squares and $\frac{2}{5}$ of the fourth square is shaded.

$$\frac{5}{5} + \frac{5}{5} + \frac{5}{5} + \frac{2}{5} = \frac{17}{5}$$

$$1 + 1 + 1 + \frac{2}{5} = 3\frac{2}{5}$$

1.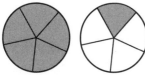

2.

3.

_____   _____   _____

Complete each table.

	Division	Improper Fraction	Mixed Number
4.	$21 \div 5$		
5.			$2\frac{3}{7}$
6.		$\frac{37}{5}$	

	Division	Improper Fraction	Mixed Number
7.		$\frac{19}{2}$	
8.			$6\frac{1}{4}$
9.	$41 \div 6$		

Problem Solving

10. Josie is ordering pizzas for the class trip. There are 14 people in Josie's class. She wants to buy enough pizzas so that each person could have $\frac{2}{6}$ of a pizza. What is the least number of pizzas Josie should order?

_____

Use with text pages 508–510.

Add and Subtract Fractions With Like Denominators

Add or subtract. Write your answer in simplest form.

$\frac{3}{8} + \frac{1}{8}$

Add the numerators. Keep the denominator the same.

$\frac{3}{8} + \frac{1}{8} = \frac{4}{8}$

Write the answer in simplest form.

$\frac{4}{8} = \frac{(4 \div 4)}{(8 \div 4)} = \frac{1}{2}$

$\frac{3}{8} + \frac{1}{8} = \frac{1}{2}$

1. $\begin{array}{r} \frac{2}{6} \\ +\frac{2}{6} \\ \hline \end{array}$

2. $\begin{array}{r} \frac{4}{7} \\ -\frac{2}{7} \\ \hline \end{array}$

3. $\begin{array}{r} \frac{5}{8} \\ +\frac{3}{8} \\ \hline \end{array}$

4. $\begin{array}{r} \frac{6}{8} \\ -\frac{2}{8} \\ \hline \end{array}$

5. $\frac{1}{7} + \frac{5}{7}$

6. $\frac{8}{12} + \frac{2}{12}$

7. $\frac{6}{9} - \frac{2}{9}$

8. $\frac{8}{12} - \frac{4}{12}$

_____ _____ _____ _____

Find the value of n.

9. $\frac{6}{10} - \frac{n}{10} = \frac{3}{10}$

10. $\frac{n}{9} + \frac{5}{9} = \frac{8}{9}$

11. $\frac{7}{8} - \frac{n}{8} = \frac{4}{8}$

_____ _____ _____

Problem Solving

12. Linda and Charlie ordered a pizza. The pizza had 8 slices. Linda ate 2 slices and Charlie ate 3 slices. What fraction of the pizza was left over?

Show your work.

_____

124

Use with text pages 516–519.

Add and Subtract Mixed Numbers

Add or subtract. Write your answer in simplest form.

$3\frac{4}{6} + 2\frac{2}{6}$	**Step 1:** Add the fractions.	**Step 2:** Add the whole numbers.
	$3\frac{4}{6}$ $+2\frac{2}{6}$ —— $\frac{6}{6}$	$3\frac{4}{6}$ $+2\frac{2}{6}$ —— $5\frac{6}{6} = 5 + 1 = 6$ $3\frac{4}{6} + 2\frac{2}{6} = 6$

1. $2\frac{2}{5}$
    $+3\frac{3}{5}$
    ——

2. $3\frac{5}{8}$
    $-2\frac{3}{8}$
    ——

3. $2\frac{4}{10}$
    $+4\frac{1}{10}$
    ——

4. $5\frac{8}{12}$
    $-1\frac{2}{12}$
    ——

5. $1\frac{5}{6}$
    $+3\frac{1}{6}$
    ——

Mental Math Is the answer a whole number? Write *yes* or *no*.

6. $3\frac{2}{7} + 1\frac{2}{7}$ 7. $5\frac{7}{8} - 2\frac{7}{8}$ 8. $3\frac{3}{5} + 5\frac{2}{5}$ 9. $6\frac{3}{4} - 2\frac{1}{4}$

_____   _____   _____   _____

Problem Solving

Show your work.

10. Ursula started with a jar that contained $4\frac{7}{8}$ cups of flour. She used $2\frac{3}{8}$ cups for a recipe. How much flour was left in the jar?

_____

125 **Use with text pages 520–521.**

Problem-Solving Application:
Decide How to Write the Quotient

Solve. Explain how you decided to write each quotient.

Mrs. Carbone asked her gym class to split up into groups of 5 students each for a relay race. The remaining students would time the race and then have a chance to race against each other. If her class has 27 students, how many groups will run the relay race? How many students will time the race?

Sometimes you need to write the remainder.

$$\begin{array}{r} 5\ R2 \\ 5\overline{)27} \\ -25 \\ \hline 2 \end{array}$$

The remainder is the number of students that timed the race.

Five groups of 5 students each will run the race and 2 students will time the race.

Show your work.

1. Misty invited 3 of her friends to help her paint her house. She bought 10 gallons of paint and split the paint equally amongst herself and her friends. How much paint did each person receive?

_____

2. Misty invited 22 guests for a scavenger hunt. She asked the guests to split into groups of 3. The remaining people would help judge the contest. How many groups went on the hunt and how many judges were there?

_____

126 **Use with text pages 522–523.**

Estimate With Fractions

Estimate each sum. Write *greater than* 1 or *less than* 1.

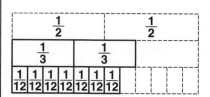

$\frac{7}{12} + \frac{2}{3}$

$\frac{7}{12}$ is greater than $\frac{1}{2}$

$\frac{2}{3}$ is greater than $\frac{1}{2}$

When both addends are greater than $\frac{1}{2}$, their sum is greater than 1.

$\frac{7}{12} + \frac{2}{3}$ is ***greater than 1.***

1. $\frac{7}{8} + \frac{8}{10}$

_____

2. $\frac{4}{9} + \frac{3}{8}$

_____

3. $\frac{3}{4} + \frac{8}{12}$

_____

4. $\frac{3}{5} + \frac{4}{7}$

_____

Estimate each sum. Write > or < for each ◯.

5. $\frac{1}{4} + \frac{2}{7}$ ◯ $\frac{6}{8} + \frac{7}{11}$

6. $\frac{5}{9} + \frac{12}{15}$ ◯ $\frac{9}{20} + \frac{6}{14}$

7. $\frac{2}{3} + \frac{7}{9}$ ◯ $\frac{4}{10} + \frac{1}{8}$

8. $\frac{5}{12} + \frac{7}{15}$ ◯ $\frac{11}{16} + \frac{5}{7}$

Problem Solving

9. Willow knitted $\frac{4}{6}$ of a square yard of fabric in the morning and $\frac{3}{4}$ of a square yard in the evening. Her sister Jessica knitted 1 whole square yard of fabric on the same day. Which sister knitted more fabric that day?

Show your work.

_____

Use with text pages 524–525.

Problem-Solving Decision: Choose a Method

Solve. Explain which method you chose.

Melissa walked $4\frac{3}{4}$ miles on Monday and $2\frac{1}{4}$ miles on Tuesday. How much farther did she walk on Monday?

Before you solve a problem with fractions, you need to decide which method to use: mental math, paper and pencil, or calculator.

The numbers are easy to compute, use mental math.

$$4\frac{3}{4} - 2\frac{1}{4} = 2\frac{2}{4}$$

Write the answer in simplest form.

$$2\frac{2}{4} = 2\frac{(2 \div 2)}{(4 \div 2)} = 2\frac{1}{2}$$

Melissa walked $2\frac{1}{2}$ miles farther on Monday.

1. Margaret walked $\frac{9}{10}$ of a kilometer before dinner and $\frac{3}{10}$ of a kilometer after dinner. How much farther did she walk before dinner?

Show your work.

_____

2. Benjamin's team lost $\frac{1}{5}$ of their basketball games last season. If his team played 20 games, how many games did the team lose?

_____

3. Julie walked $9\frac{4}{10}$ miles the first week of June, $5\frac{7}{10}$ miles the second week, $10\frac{5}{10}$ miles the third week, and $8\frac{2}{10}$ miles the last week in June. How many miles did she walk in June?

_____

Use with text pages 526–527.

Add Fractions With Unlike Denominators

Find each sum. Use fraction strips to help you.

$\frac{1}{3} + \frac{1}{6}$

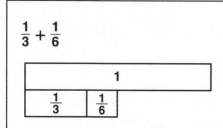

Find like fraction strips that fit exactly under $\frac{1}{3} + \frac{1}{6}$.

$\frac{1}{3} + \frac{1}{6} = \frac{3}{6} = \frac{1}{2}$

1. $\frac{7}{8} + \frac{1}{4}$

2. $\frac{2}{3} + \frac{7}{12}$

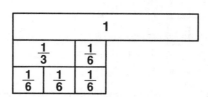

_____

_____

3. $\frac{3}{4} + \frac{11}{12}$

4. $\frac{3}{4} + \frac{1}{2}$

5. $\frac{3}{16} + \frac{1}{4}$

_____

_____

_____

Problem Solving

6. Kevin drew a square and cut the square into 12 equal parts. Tyler drew a congruent square and cut the square into 4 equal parts. Write a fraction problem that would represent adding 9 parts from Kevin's square and 1 part from Tyler's square. Solve the problem.

_____ Date _____

Use with text pages 528–529.

Subtract Fractions With Unlike Denominators

Use fraction strips to help you find each difference.

$\frac{3}{4} - \frac{1}{6}$

$\frac{1}{4}$	$\frac{1}{4}$	$\frac{1}{4}$

| $\frac{1}{6}$ | ? | |

Make fraction strips using equivalent fractions.

$\frac{3}{4} = \frac{9}{12}$ and $\frac{1}{6} = \frac{2}{12}$

$\frac{9}{12} - \frac{2}{12} = \frac{7}{12}$

$\frac{3}{4} - \frac{1}{6} = \frac{7}{12}$

$\frac{1}{12}$	$\frac{1}{12}$	$\frac{1}{12}$	$\frac{1}{12}$	$\frac{1}{12}$	$\frac{1}{12}$	$\frac{1}{12}$	$\frac{1}{12}$	$\frac{1}{12}$

$\frac{1}{12}$	$\frac{1}{12}$	?

Find like fraction strips that fit exactly in the remaining space.

1. $\frac{11}{12} - \frac{1}{4}$

2. $\frac{1}{4} - \frac{1}{6}$

3. $\frac{9}{12} - \frac{2}{3}$

4. $\frac{1}{3} - \frac{1}{12}$

5. $\frac{4}{5} - \frac{5}{10}$

_____

_____

_____

_____

_____

6. $\frac{9}{10} - \frac{1}{2}$

7. $\frac{2}{4} - \frac{2}{6}$

8. $\frac{7}{8} - \frac{5}{16}$

9. $\frac{2}{10} - \frac{1}{5}$

10. $\frac{5}{8} - \frac{1}{2}$

_____

_____

_____

_____

_____

Problem Solving

11. Betty lined up three different fraction strips to fit exactly under $\frac{11}{12}$. One of the fraction strips is a $\frac{1}{2}$ strip. What are the other two fraction strips?

_____

Use with text pages 530–532.

Problem-Solving Application: Use Circle Graphs

Mrs. Lucille gave 60 students the choice of four different activities during recess time. The circle graph shows what fractions of the students chose to play racing, dodge ball, kick ball, or hide and seek. Use the circle graph to solve each problem.

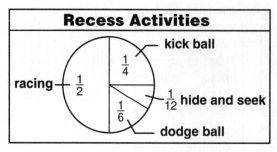

Recess Activities

kick ball $\frac{1}{4}$
racing $\frac{1}{2}$
$\frac{1}{6}$
$\frac{1}{12}$ hide and seek
dodge ball

How many more students chose kick ball than dodge ball?

Find out how many students chose kick ball and how many students chose dodge ball.

$$\text{kick ball} = \frac{1}{4} \text{ of } 60 = 15 \text{ students}$$

$$\text{dodge ball} = \frac{1}{6} \text{ of } 60 = 10 \text{ students}$$

Find the difference.
$15 - 10 = 5$

Five more students chose kick ball than dodge ball.

---

1. How many students chose either racing or hide and seek?

_____

Show your work.

2. Suppose that there are 96 students instead of 60, but the graph is the same. How many students chose dodge ball?

_____

Use with text pages 534–536.

Tenths and Hundredths

Write a fraction and a decimal to describe each model.

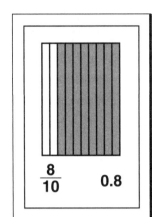

$\frac{8}{10}$ 0.8

1.

_____

_____

2.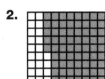

_____

_____

3.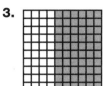

_____

_____

Use grid paper. Draw a model to show each fraction. Then write each fraction as a decimal.

4. $\frac{6}{10}$ **5.** $\frac{40}{100}$ **6.** $\frac{7}{10}$ **7.** $\frac{92}{100}$ **8.** $\frac{63}{100}$

_____   _____   _____   _____   _____

Use grid paper. Draw a model to show each decimal. Then write each decimal as a fraction.

9. 0.8   **10.** 0.46   **11.** 0.3   **12.** 0.33   **13.** 0.66

_____   _____   _____   _____   _____

Problem Solving

14. Lucy writes the number $\frac{67}{100}$. Taylor writes the number 0.7. Are the numbers equivalent? Explain your answer.

_____

_____

_____

_____

           Use with text pages 542–543.

Thousandths

Write each as a decimal.

$\dfrac{27}{1,000}$

The decimal is 27 thousandths.

$\dfrac{27}{1,000} = 0.027$

1. $\dfrac{8}{1,000}$

_____

2. $\dfrac{30}{1,000}$

_____

3. $\dfrac{700}{1,000}$

_____

4. 321 thousandths

_____

5. 6 thousandths

_____

6. 38 thousandths

_____

Write each in word form.

7. $\dfrac{4}{1,000}$

_____

_____

8. 0.047

_____

_____

9. 0.003

_____

_____

10. 0.384

_____

_____

_____

11. $\dfrac{555}{1,000}$

_____

_____

_____

12. 0.627

_____

_____

_____

Problem Solving

Show your work.

13. Gerald walked $\dfrac{6}{10}$ miles to the market. Later in the day he walked 0.640 miles to his cousin's house. Which walk was longer? Explain how you know.

_____

_____

_____

_____

Use with text pages 544–545.

Mixed Numbers and Decimals

Write each as a decimal.

$4\frac{5}{10}$

The mixed number shows 4 and 5 tenths.

$4\frac{5}{10} = 4.5$

1. $5\frac{9}{10}$ **2.** $7\frac{654}{1,000}$ **3.** $3\frac{86}{100}$

_____   _____   _____

Write each as a decimal in standard form.

4. seven and forty-four thousandths _____

5. $3 + 0.8 + 0.04 + 0.007$ _____

6. $10 + 0.4 + 0.03 + 0.002$ _____

Write each decimal in words and in expanded form.

7. 0.645 _____

_____

8. 7.034 _____

_____

9. 5.24 _____

_____

Problem Solving

Show your work.

10. Missy writes the number $6\frac{60}{100}$. Jessica writes the number 6.6. Marion writes the number "six and six tenths." Joseph writes $6 + 0.6$. Did each student write the same number? Explain.

_____

Use with text pages 546–548.

Fractions and Decimal Equivalents

Write each decimal as an equivalent fraction.

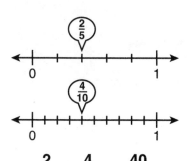

0.4
You can use number lines.

$0.4 = \frac{2}{5}$ or $\frac{4}{10}$ or $\frac{40}{100}$

1. 0.74 _____

2. 0.31 _____

3. 0.062 _____

4. 0.59 _____

Write each fraction as an equivalent decimal.

5. $\frac{3}{5}$ _____

6. $\frac{1}{4}$ _____

7. $\frac{13}{20}$ _____

8. $\frac{19}{25}$ _____

9. $\frac{450}{1,000}$ _____

Find the missing digit.

10. $\frac{74}{1000} = .0\blacksquare4$

11. $\frac{\blacksquare5}{100} = .15$

12. $4\frac{7}{\blacksquare0} = 4.7$

Problem Solving

13. Suppose there are 1,000 marbles and $\frac{3}{4}$ of the marbles are colors other than black. If the rest of them are black, how many marbles are black? Explain how you found your answer.

_____

_____

Use with text pages 550–552.

Problem-Solving Strategy:
Find a Pattern

Find a pattern to solve each problem.

Look at this pattern of numbers.

$$7 \quad 12 \quad 18 \quad 25 \quad 33 \quad 42 \quad 52 \quad 63$$

If the pattern continues, what is the next number likely to be?

What is the difference between each number and the following number?

$$7 + \mathbf{5} = 12$$
$$12 + \mathbf{6} = 18$$
$$18 + \mathbf{7} = 25$$
$$25 + \mathbf{8} = 33$$
$$33 + \mathbf{9} = 42$$
$$42 + \mathbf{10} = 52$$
$$52 + \mathbf{11} = 63$$

Use the pattern to find the next number.

$$63 + \mathbf{12} = 75$$

The next number is 75.

1. One book sells for $8, two books sell for $15.50, and three books sell for $22.50. If the pattern continues, how many books can you buy for $35?

Show your work.

_____

2. Look at this pattern of numbers.

$$91 \quad 82 \quad 73 \quad 64 \quad 55 \quad 46 \quad 37$$

If the pattern continues, what is the next number likely to be?

_____

Use with text pages 554–556.

Compare and Order Decimals

Compare. Write >, <, or = for each ◯.

3.79 ◯ 3.97

You can use a place-value chart.

ones		tenths	hundredths
3	.	7	9
3	.	9	7

Compare the numbers, starting from the left.

7 < 9, so **3.79 < 3.97**

---

1. 23.23 ◯ 23.32   **2.** 7.8 ◯ 8.07

3. 6.600 ◯ 6.006   **4.** 12.40 ◯ 12.4

5. 5.01 ◯ 4.99   **6.** 18.5 ◯ 20.2   **7.** 12.47 ◯ 12.74   **8.** 9.56 ◯ 9.65

Order the numbers from least to greatest.

9. 38.42 3.842 0.384 3.084   **10.** 5.40 5.54 5.045 5.45

_____   _____

11. 7.59 7.05 57.01 7.95   **12.** 16.54 1.654 1.665 16.45

_____   _____

Problem Solving

13. Four gymnastics competitors have scores of 9.73, 9.89, 9.8, and 9.79. What is the order of the scores from least to greatest? Explain how you found your answer.

_____

_____

_____

137   **Use with text pages 558–559.**

Compare and Order Decimals and Mixed Numbers

Compare. Write >, <, or = for each ◯.

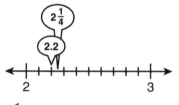

$2\frac{1}{4}$ ◯ **2.2.**

You can use a number line.

$2\frac{1}{4}$ is to the right of 2.2, so $2\frac{1}{4}$ **> 2.2**

1. 5.2 ◯ $5\frac{2}{5}$ **2.** 37.42 ◯ $37\frac{42}{1,000}$

3. $6\frac{3}{4}$ ◯ 6.75   **4.** 8.054 ◯ $8\frac{54}{100}$

Order the numbers from greatest to least.

5. $3\frac{4}{5}$ 3.45   3.054 $3\frac{54}{100}$

_____

6. 10.001   1.01 $10\frac{1}{100}$ $10\frac{1}{10}$

_____

7. 8.45   8.04 $8\frac{45}{1000}$ $8\frac{4}{1000}$

_____

8. $\frac{351}{1000}$ .03   .65 $\frac{39}{100}$

_____

Write > or < for each ◯.

9. 7.6 ◯ 7.67 ◯ 7.07   **10.** 5.32 ◯ 5.033 ◯ 5.34

11. 3.5 ◯ 3.501 ◯ 3.05   **12.** 7.995 ◯ 7.986 ◯ 8.01

Problem Solving

13. A file clerk was asked to put the following codes in order from least to greatest: 2.82, $2\frac{4}{5}$, 2.083, $2\frac{84}{100}$. How should the codes be ordered?

_____

Use with text pages 560–562.

Round Decimals

Round each decimal to the nearest tenth.

9.75

```
Rounding Rules:

   Step 1          Step 2          Step 3
Find the place   Look at the     Round as
you want to      digit to the    you do with
round to.        right.          whole
   9.75            9.75          numbers.

                                  5 ≥ 5

9.75 rounds to 9.8.            Increase the
                               tenths digit
                               by one.
```

1. 4.812   2. 7.234   3. 53.327   4. 20.481   5. 19.937

_____   _____   _____   _____   _____

6. 35.781   7. 401.87   8. 48.614   9. 1,687.12   10. 9.187

_____   _____   _____   _____   _____

Round each decimal to the place of the underlined digit.

11. 4<u>7</u>.81   12. <u>8</u>.8   13. 7.<u>8</u>1   14. 6<u>7</u>.18   15. 51.<u>9</u>0

_____   _____   _____   _____   _____

16. 4<u>5</u>.83   17. 95<u>8</u>.66   18. 14.6<u>2</u>1   19. 578.1<u>9</u>6   20. 64.7<u>4</u>9

_____   _____   _____   _____   _____

Problem Solving

21. Kim filled her car with 7.38 gallons of gasoline. How much gas did she buy to the nearest whole gallon?

_____

Use with text pages 568–569.

Estimate Decimal Sums and Differences

Estimate by rounding to the nearest whole number.

$7.5 \rightarrow \quad 8$ $\underline{+\ 3.8} \rightarrow \underline{+4}$ $\qquad\qquad 12$ $7.5 + 3.8 \approx 12$	Add the rounded numbers.

1. 8.1
 $\underline{-6.6}$

2. $44.87
 $\underline{+\ 58.16}$

3. $72.38
 $\underline{-\ 60.08}$

4.   75.84
 $\underline{-30.41}$

5.   22.987
 $\underline{+\ 6.287}$

6.   546.8
 $\underline{-321.3}$

7. $309.55
 $\underline{+\ 68.41}$

8. $365.27
 $\underline{-\ 195.88}$

9. $917.35 + $342.32

_____

10. $463.84 − $283.24

_____

11. $583.37 + $418.94

_____

12. $729.54 + $186.34

_____

13. $741.65 − $387.14

_____

14. $612.99 + $257.64

_____

Problem Solving

Show your work.

15. Kevin needs to fix a flat tire on his bicycle. He bought an inner tube for $8.79 and a patch kit for $3.28. About how much did he spend in all? Round each amount to the nearest whole dollar.

_____

Use with text pages 570–571.

Probability as a Fraction

For each spinner, write the probability that a spin will land
on a shaded region. Write the probability in both words and
fraction form.

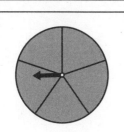

1.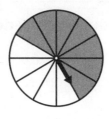

_____

2.

_____

3.

_____

The probability
is 5 out of 5 or
1 out of 1. As a
fraction, it is $\frac{5}{5}$
or 1.

Write the probability of each event in both words and
fraction form.

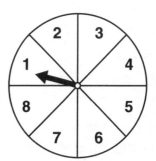

4. spinning 7, 3, or 2

_____

5. spinning a multiple of 2

_____

Problem Solving

6. A bag holds 3 yellow marbles and 7 blue
marbles. How many and what color marbles
could you add to the bag so that the probability
of picking a yellow marble is $\frac{1}{4}$?

Show your work.

_____

145 **Use with text pages 598–600.**

Make Predictions

A cube has its faces labeled with the following letters: A, B, C, A, B, A. Use this cube to solve each problem.

Predict how many times the cube will land on the letter B if you toss the cube 60 times.

Step 1 Find the probability of rolling the letter B once.
Letter B → 2 out of 6 = $\frac{1}{3}$

Step 2 Predict the number of times the cube will land on letter B.
Letter B → $\frac{1}{3}$ of 60 = 20 rolls

It is probable that 20 rolls out of 60 rolls will land on the letter B.

---

1. Predict how many times the cube will land on the letter C if you toss the cube 30 times.

_____

2. Predict how many times the cube will land on the letter A if you toss the cube 20 times.

_____

3. Predict how many times the cube will land on the letter B if you toss the cube 150 times.

_____

4. Suppose one of the faces with an "A" was changed to a "D". Predict how many times the new cube will land on the letter A if you toss it 480 times.

_____

Problem Solving

5. A bag holds 6 yellow marbles and 4 blue marbles. Predict how many times you would pick out a yellow marble, if you picked out a marble and put it back into the bag 75 times.

_____

Show your work.

Use with text pages 602–603.

Problem-Solving Strategy:
Make an Organized List

Make an organized list to solve each problem.

> **Tony, Dale, Walter, and Blake are in line at a movie theater. How many ways can the boys be arranged if Dale has to be first in line?**
>
> Make an organized list of all the possible arrangements.
>
> Dale, Tony, Walter, Blake
> Dale, Tony, Blake, Walter
> Dale, Walter, Tony, Blake
> Dale, Walter, Blake, Tony
> Dale, Blake, Tony, Walter
> Dale, Blake, Walter, Tony
>
> **The boys can be arranged 6 different ways.**

1. Joel is using the digits 1, 4, 5, and 8 to make as many four-digit numbers as he can. What are all the numbers Joel can make?

Show your work.

2. Eric is rearranging the letters of his first name. How many different ways can he rearrange the letters of his name? Include his name in the list.

_____

3. Vivian, Haley, and Tracy are having a race. If they line up in a row at the starting line, how many different ways can they arrange themselves from left to right?

_____

Find Probability

Use the spinner to solve each problem.

If you spin the spinner two times, what is the probability that the spinner will land on the black region twice?

| You can use a grid. | | | | Count the number of outcomes that have black two times. |

Second Spin

		black	white	striped
First Spin	**black**	black, black	black, white	black, striped
	white	white, black	white, white	white, striped
	striped	striped, black	striped, white	striped, striped

Count the number of outcomes that have black two times.

The probability of landing on black twice is $\frac{1}{9}$.

---

1. What is the probability of one spin landing on the white area and one spin landing on the black area?

_____

2. What is the probability that one of the spins will land on the white area and that the other will not land on the white area?

_____

Problem Solving

3. Make a tree diagram or a grid to show the possible outcomes of two consecutive spins if the spinner had 4 equal parts that are red, blue, yellow, and green.

Use with text pages 608–610.

Locate Points on a Grid

Write the letter of the point for each ordered pair.

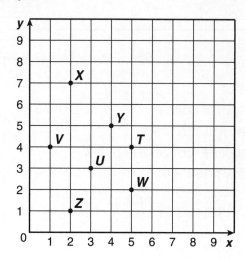

(5, 4)	
Start at 0.	
Move right 5 units.	
Then move up 4 units.	
Point *T* is at (5, 4).	

1. (1, 4) **2.** (2, 7) **3.** (2, 1)

_____   _____   _____

Write the ordered pair for each point.

4. *U*   **5.** *W*   **6.** *Y*

_____   _____   _____

7. Which coordinates of point *X* and point *Z* are the same? Which are different?

_____

_____

8. Write directions explaining how to plot point *X*.

_____

_____

Problem Solving

9. Write directions for locating a point whose coordinates are (3, 10).

_____

_____

149 **Use with text pages 616–617.**

Graph Ordered Pairs

Plot each point and label it with the correct letter on the grid.

Z (3, 5)

- Start at 0.
- Move right 3 units.
- Then move up 5 units.
- Then make a dot on the point.
- Label the point *Z*.

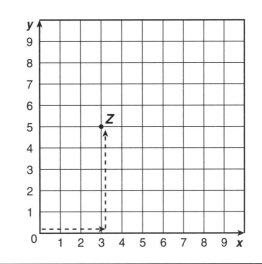

1. *A* (1, 3)	**2.** *B* (3, 2)
3. *C* (4, 4)	**4.** *D* (2, 5)
5. *E* (0, 6)	**6.** *F* (6, 3)
7. *G* (5, 0)	**8.** *H* (2, 1)
9. *I* (4, 1)	**10.** *J* (2, 2)

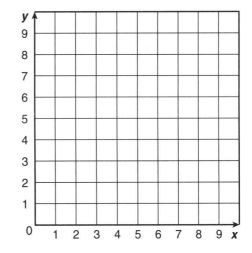

Problem Solving

11. Beth collected data on how many hours she spent on chores each day. She made a line graph of the data. Complete the table, using the day as the first coordinate and the number of hours as the second coordinate.

Chores	
Day	Hours

Chores

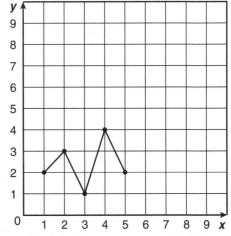

Use with text pages 618–619.

Algebra: Graph Functions

Boxes of Plates $y = 3x$	
Number of boxes (x)	Number of plates (y)
1	3
2	6
3	9
4	12
5	15
6	18

Sarah is packing plates into boxes. Each box can fit 3 plates. She wants to know how many plates are in 6 boxes.

Find the number of plates by graphing the function $y = 3x$.

Step 1: Plot and **connect** the points from the table. Use the number of boxes as the x-coordinate and the number of plates as the y-coordinate.

Step 2: Extend the line segment to see how many plates will fit into larger numbers of boxes. The points should lie on a line.

Step 3: Find the point on the line for 6 boxes. Start at 0 and move 6 units to the right to match the number of boxes. Then move up to the meet the line at (6,18).

There are 18 plates in 6 boxes.

1. Extend the graph. Find the number of plates in 8 boxes.

_____

2. Thirty-six plates are in boxes. How many boxes were used.

_____

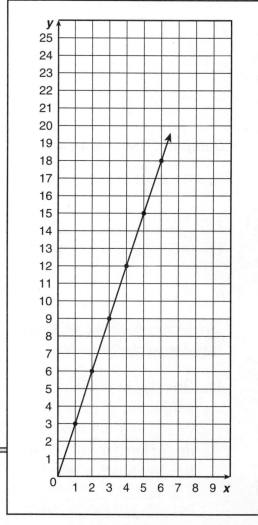

Problem Solving

3. Name three points that would lie on the line graphed by the function $y = 8x$.

_____

Use with text pages 620–622.

Integers

For each letter, write the integer from the number line.

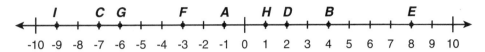

```
     I    C G      F    A    H D    B        E
  ◄──┼──┼──┼──┼──┼──┼──┼──┼──┼──┼──┼──┼──┼──┼──┼──┼──┼──┼──┼──┼──►
   -10 -9 -8 -7 -6 -5 -4 -3 -2 -1  0  1  2  3  4  5  6  7  8  9  10
```

H

Point *H* is located 1 unit to the right of 0. It is a positive integer.

H = 1

1. *E* _____

2. *D* _____

3. *C* _____

4. *I* _____

5. *F* _____

6. *A* _____

7. *G* _____

8. *B* _____

Compare. Use >, <, or = for each ◯.

9. +1 ◯ 1

10. −7 ◯ 4

11. 3 ◯ +2

12. −3 ◯ 1

13. 0 ◯ −9

14. 5 ◯ +5

15. −7 ◯ −1

16. −3 ◯ 3

Problem Solving

17. One day in Burlington, Vermont, the temperature ranged from −12 to −4. Which was the low temperature for the day? How far from 0 was the high temperature?

Show your work.

_____

152

Use with text pages 624–626.

Problem-Solving Application:
Use a Graph

The local movie theater is having a deal for matinee movies.
The first person in a group pays full price, and each other
person in the group gets a discount. The graph shows the
relationship between the number of people in a group and the
cost of their tickets. Use the graph to solve each problem.

**How much will it cost 3 for people to see
the matinee movie?**

Find 3 on the *x*-axis and then draw an arrow
up to meet the graphed line.

**It will cost $14 for 3 people to see the
matinee movie.**

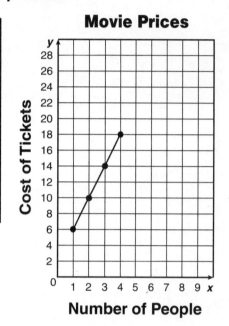

Movie Prices

Number of People

1. How much more would it cost for 8
   people to see the matinee movie than
   for 4 people to see the matinee movie?

   _____

Show your work.

2. A group of people spent a total of $22
   on tickets and snacks for the matinee
   movie. If the group spent $8 on
   snacks, how many people were in the
   group?

   _____

3. John has $60 to spend on matinee
   tickets. What is the greatest number of
   people including himself that he can
   buy tickets for? How much money will
   he have left?

   _____

153   **Use with text pages 628–630.**